Welcome To
Feathers & Fur
Adult Coloring Book vol. 1

By CreaTiv Books

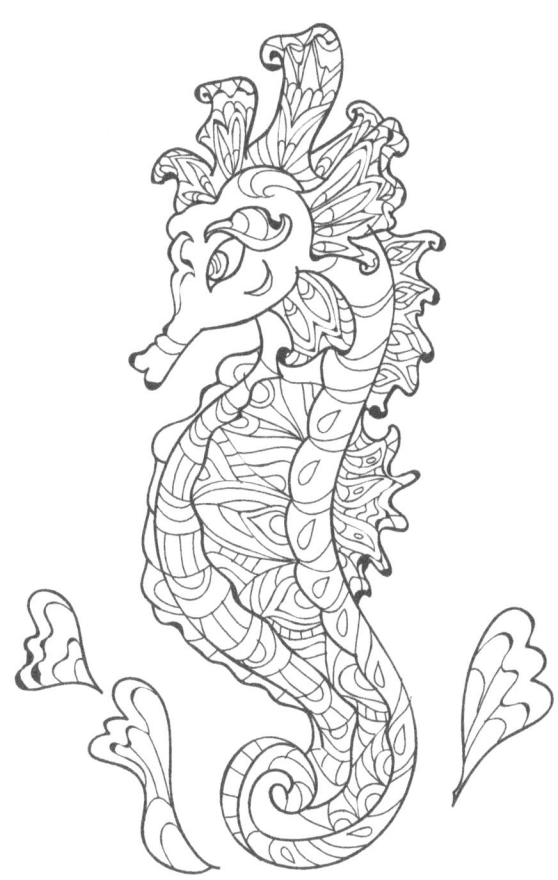

www.creativbooks.com

The pages in this book are suitable for colored pencils, markers and a variety of other media. To help prevent bleed through, please place a blank piece of paper underneath the page that you are coloring on.

1. Break out your colored pencils or fine point markers and choose a page.

2. Let your mind drift away as you begin to color.

3. Express yourself in the colors you choose.

4. Stop when you feel the need.

5. Return the next day for more :)

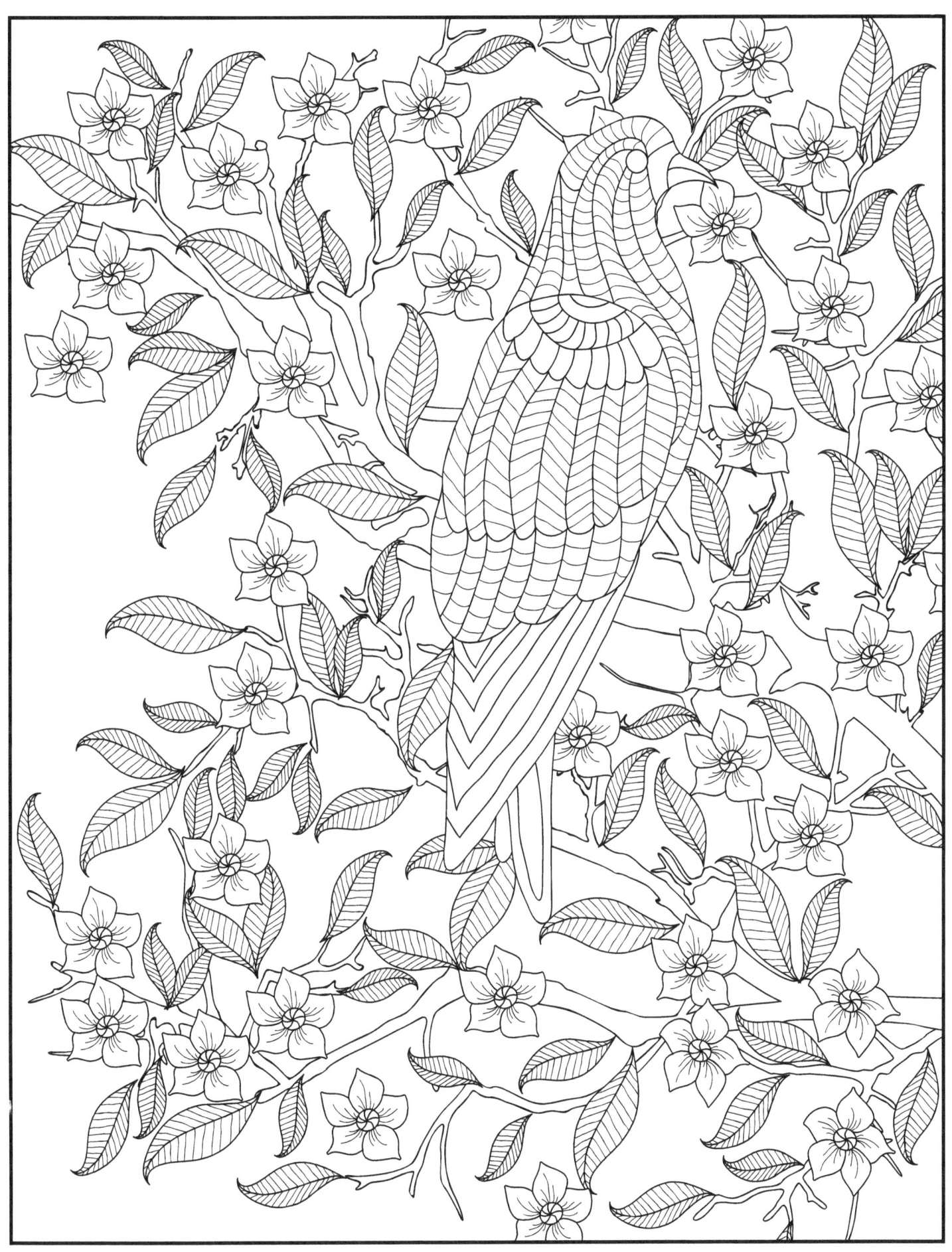

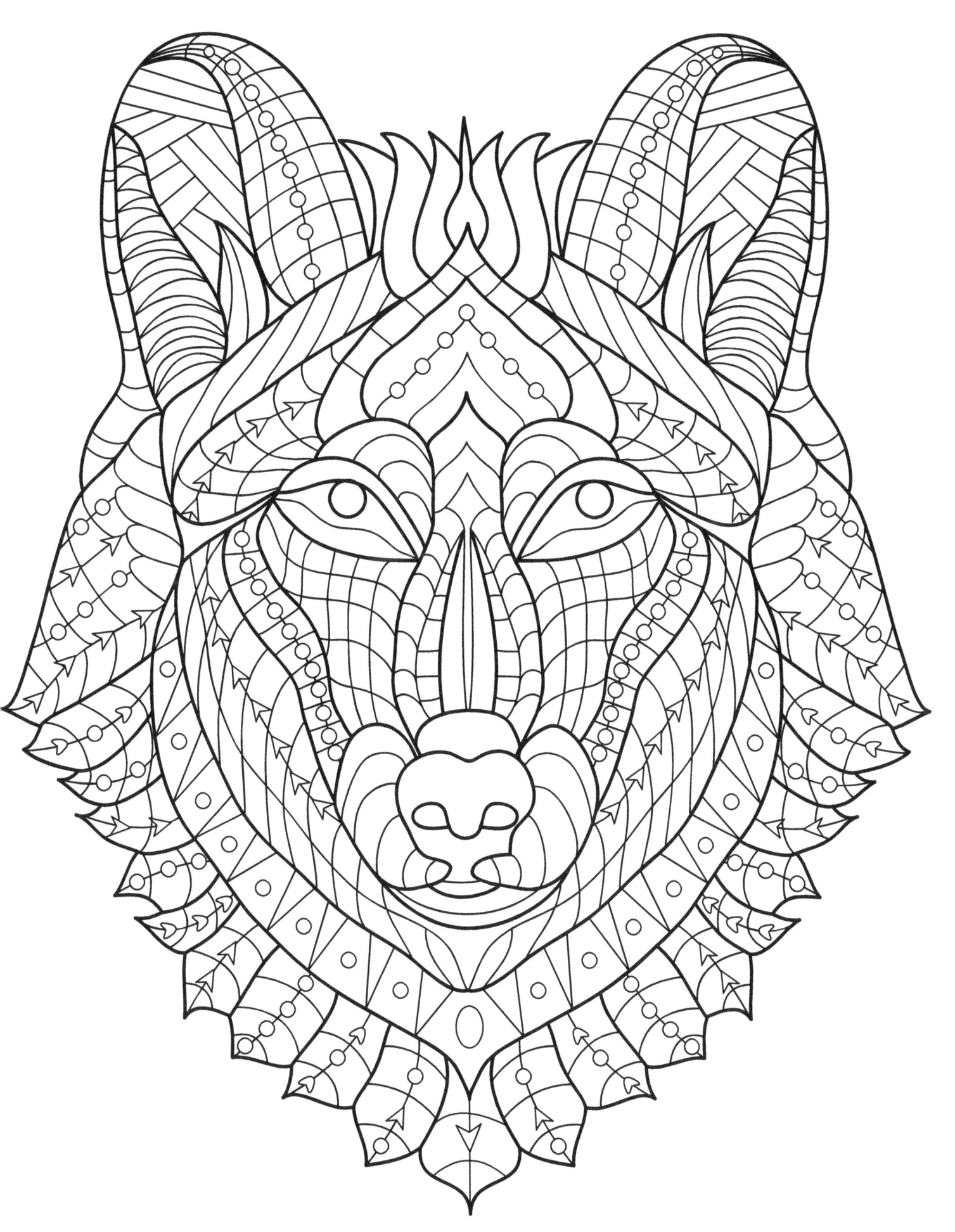

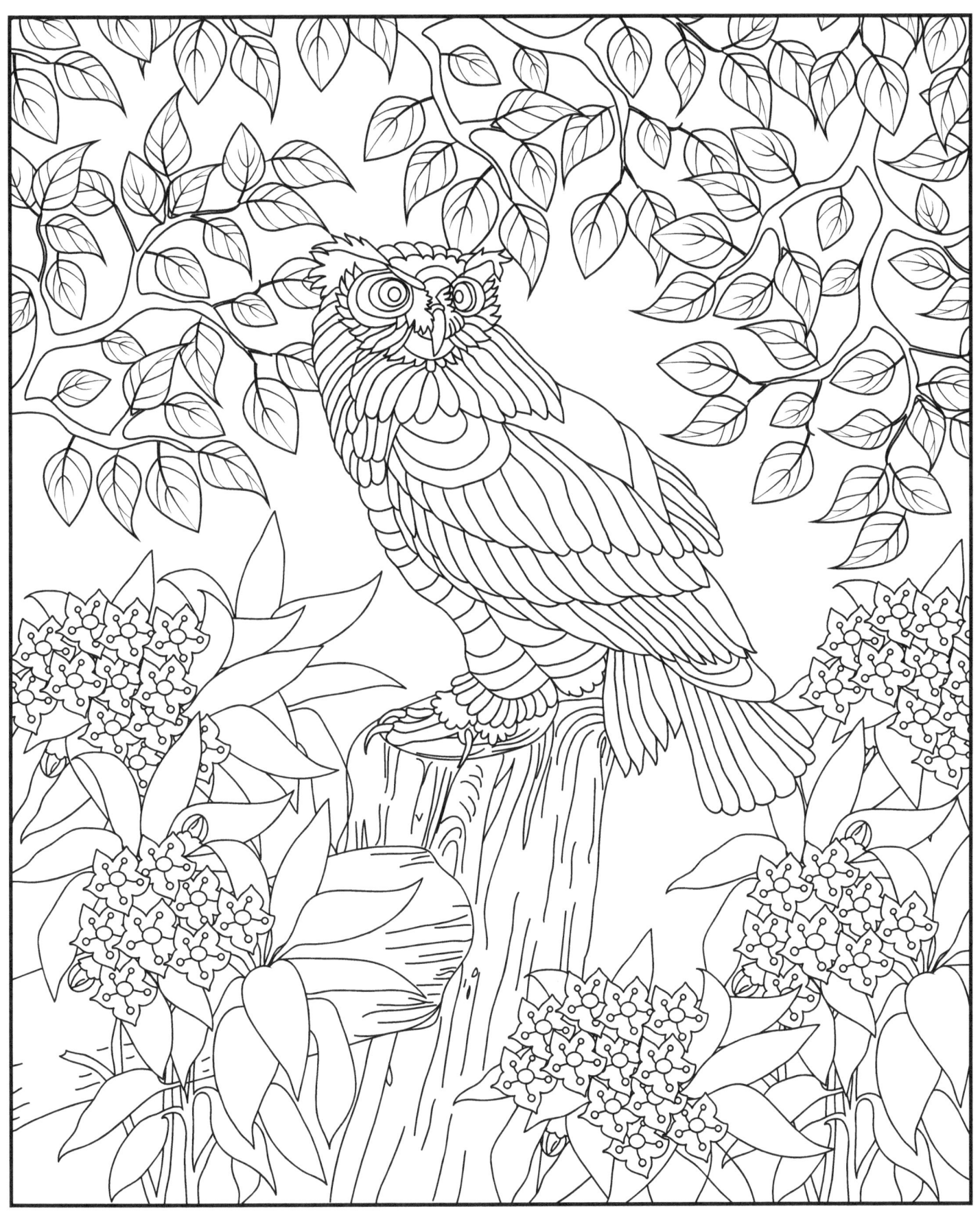

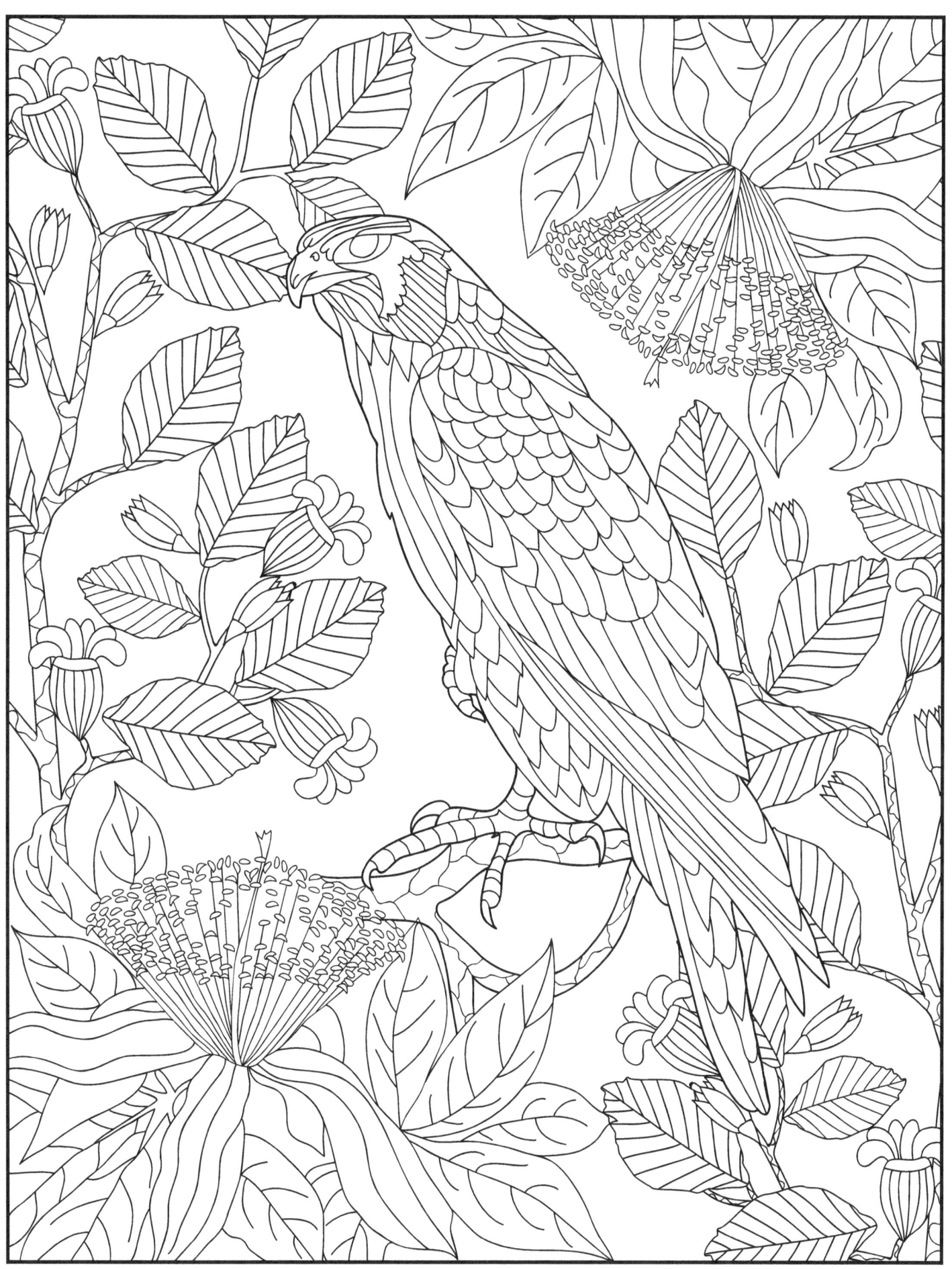

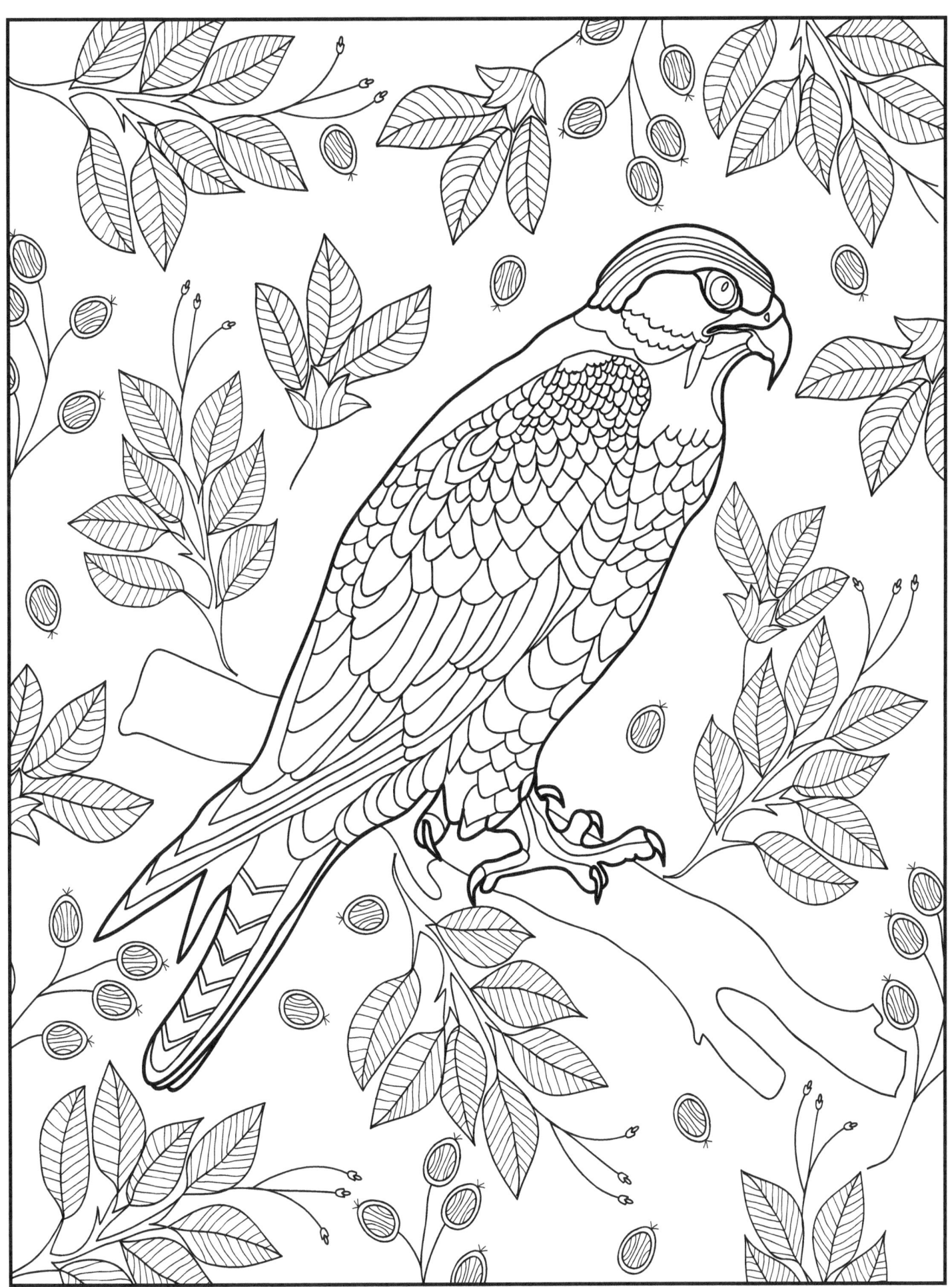

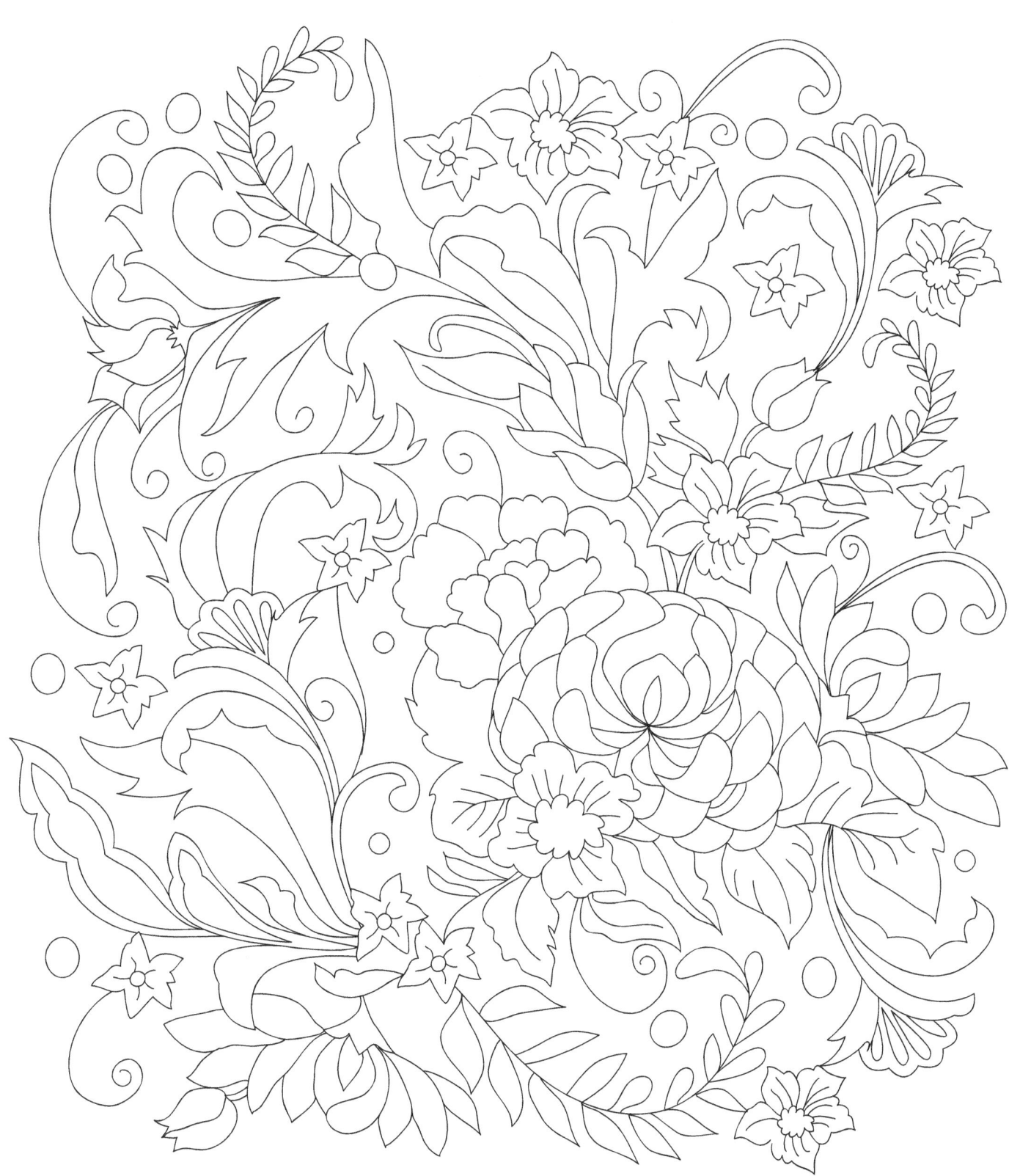

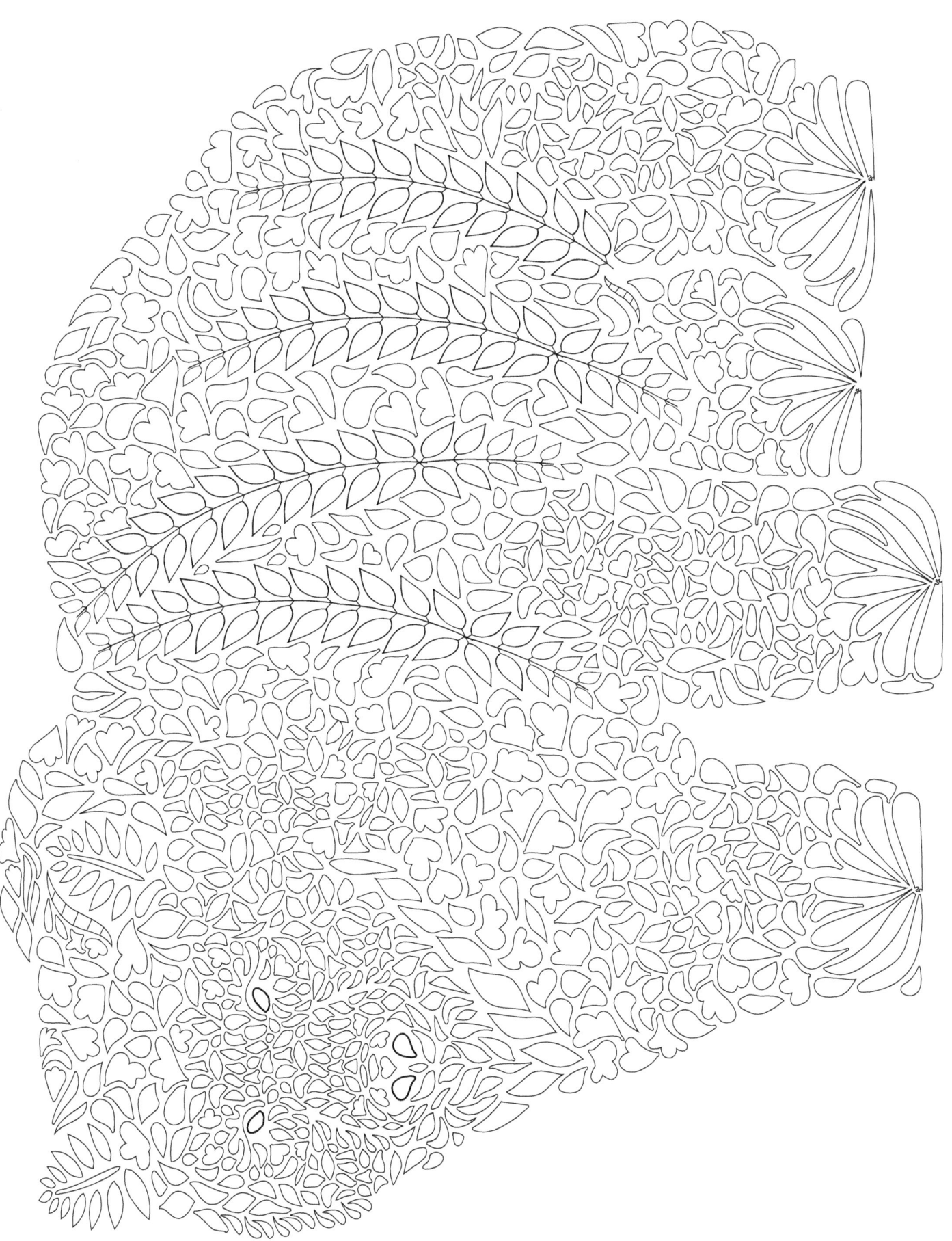

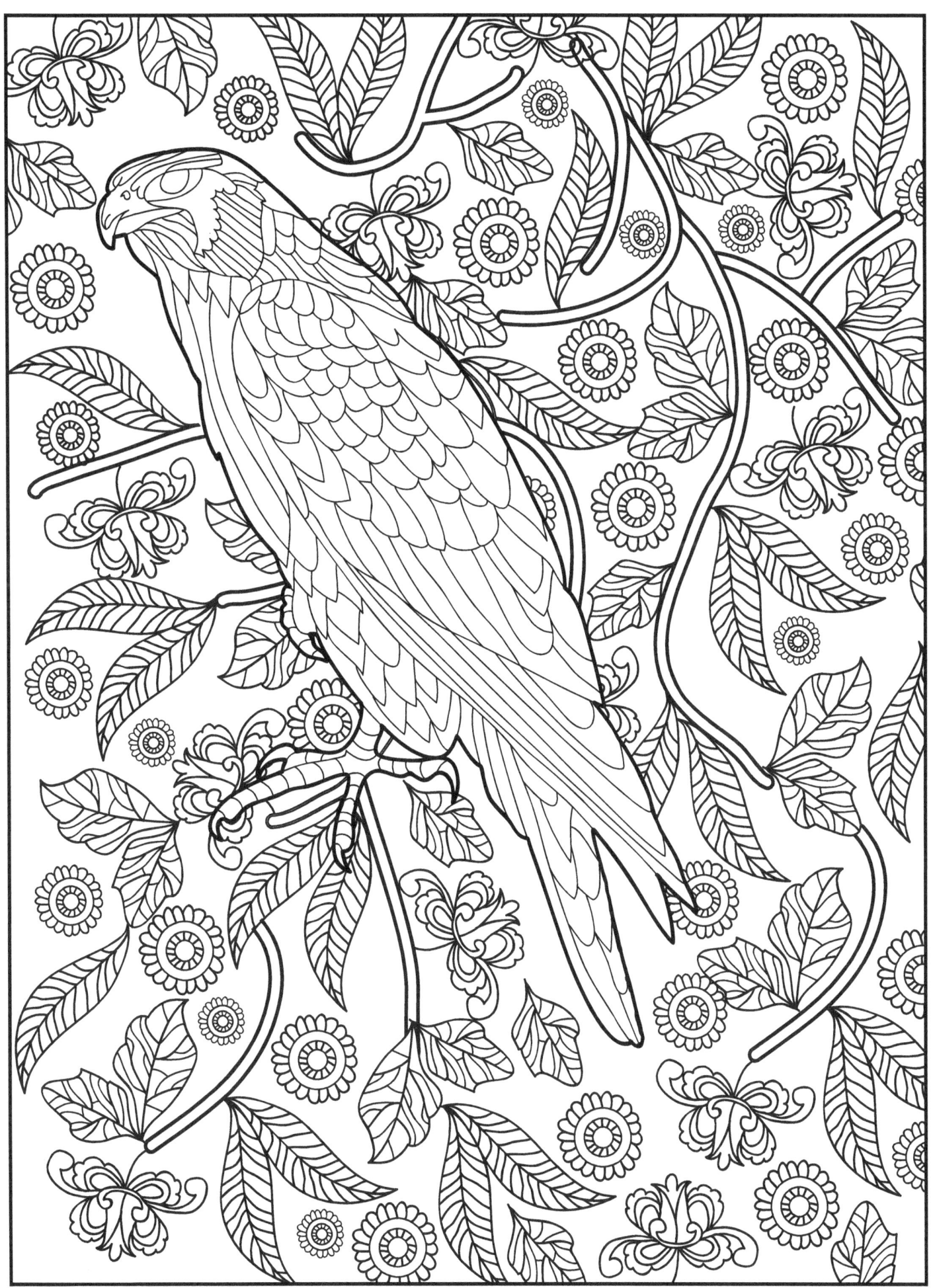

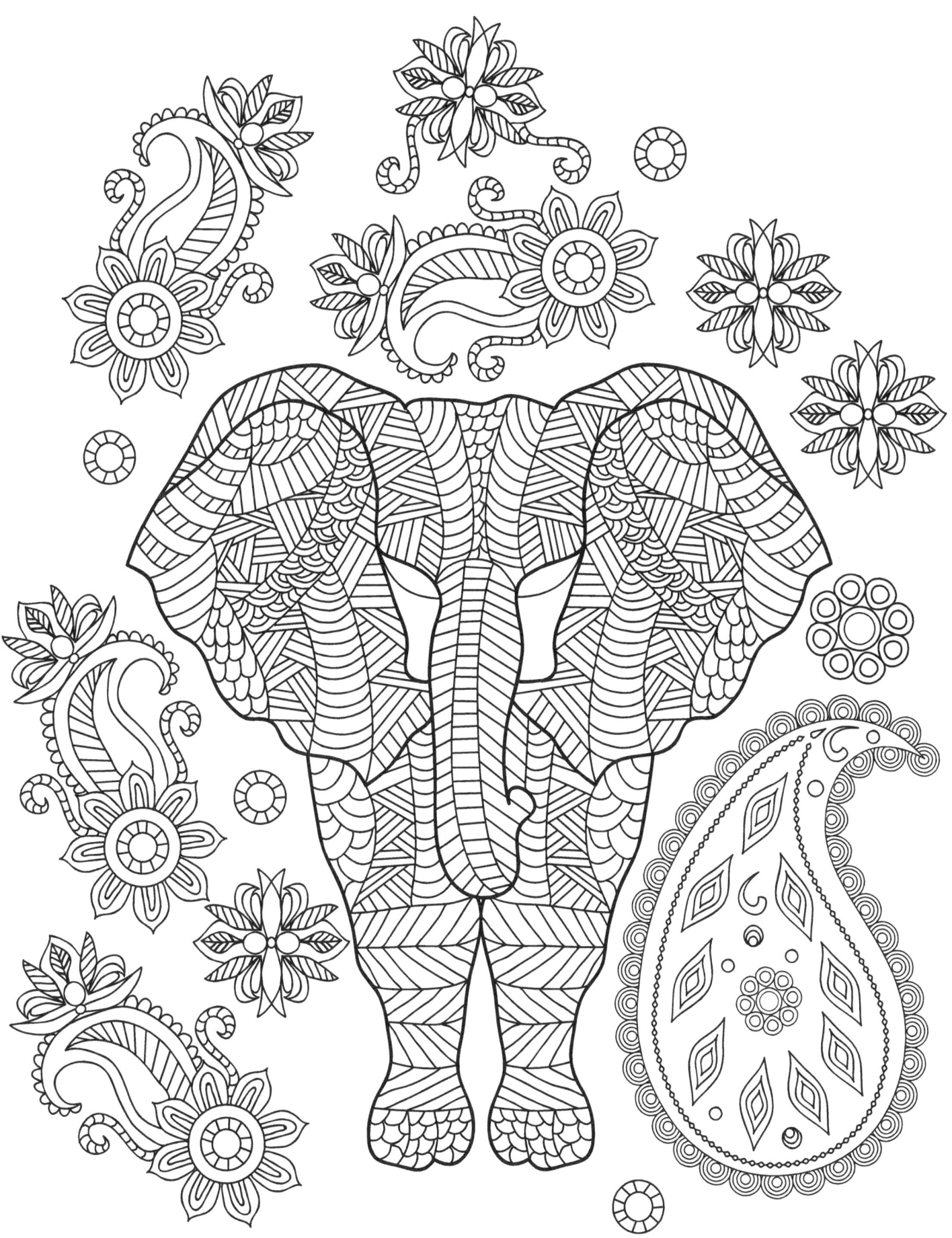

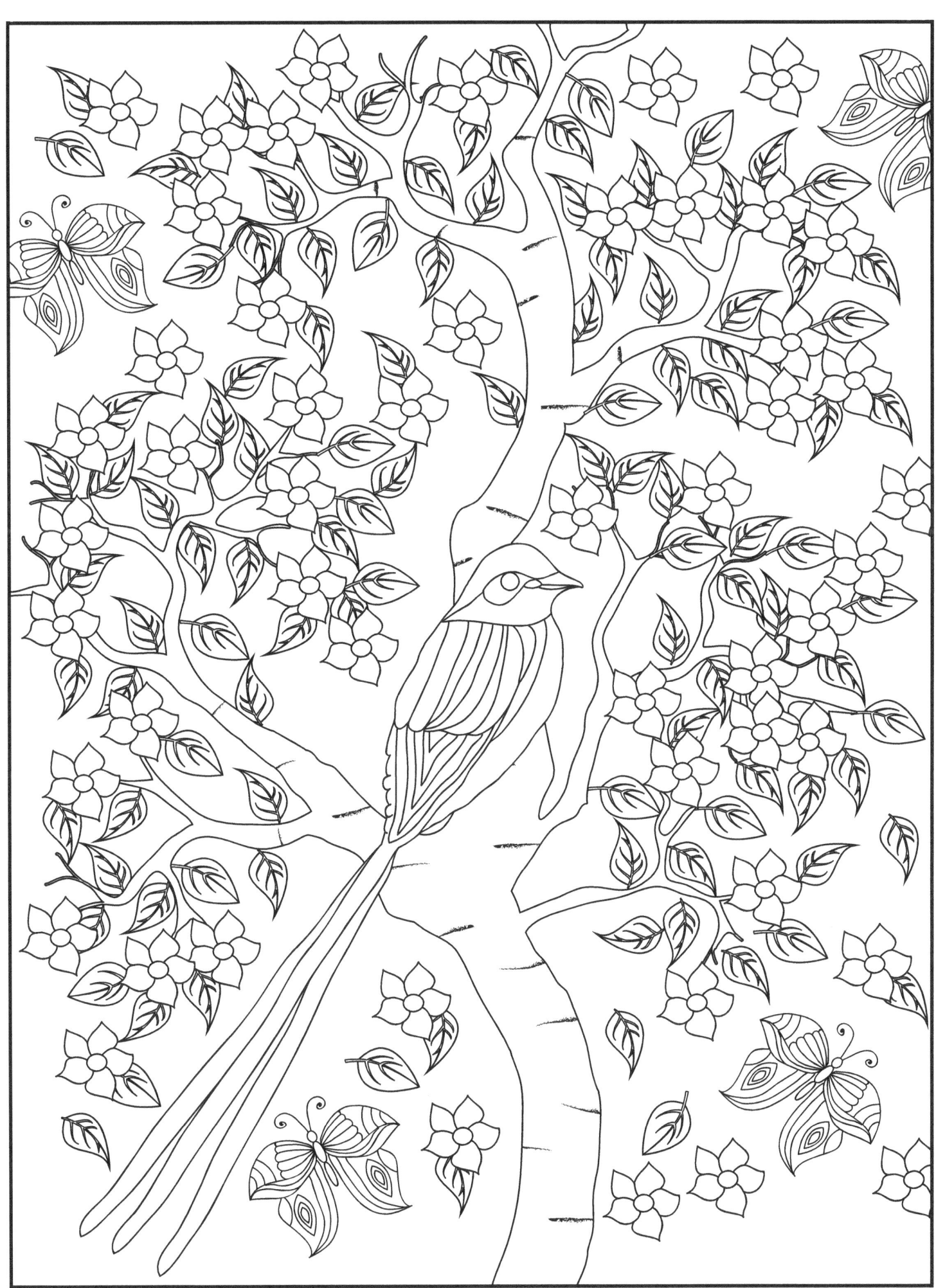

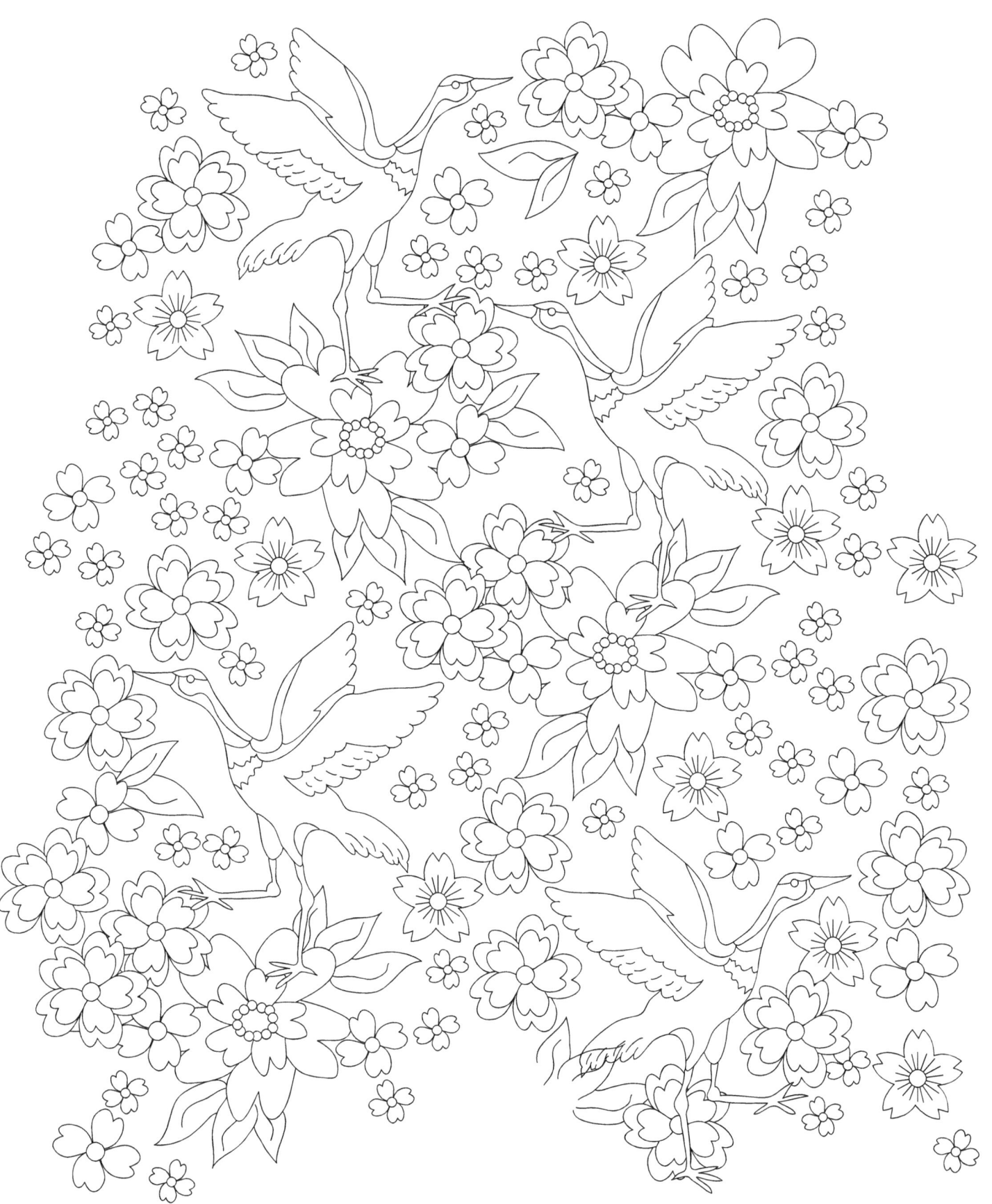

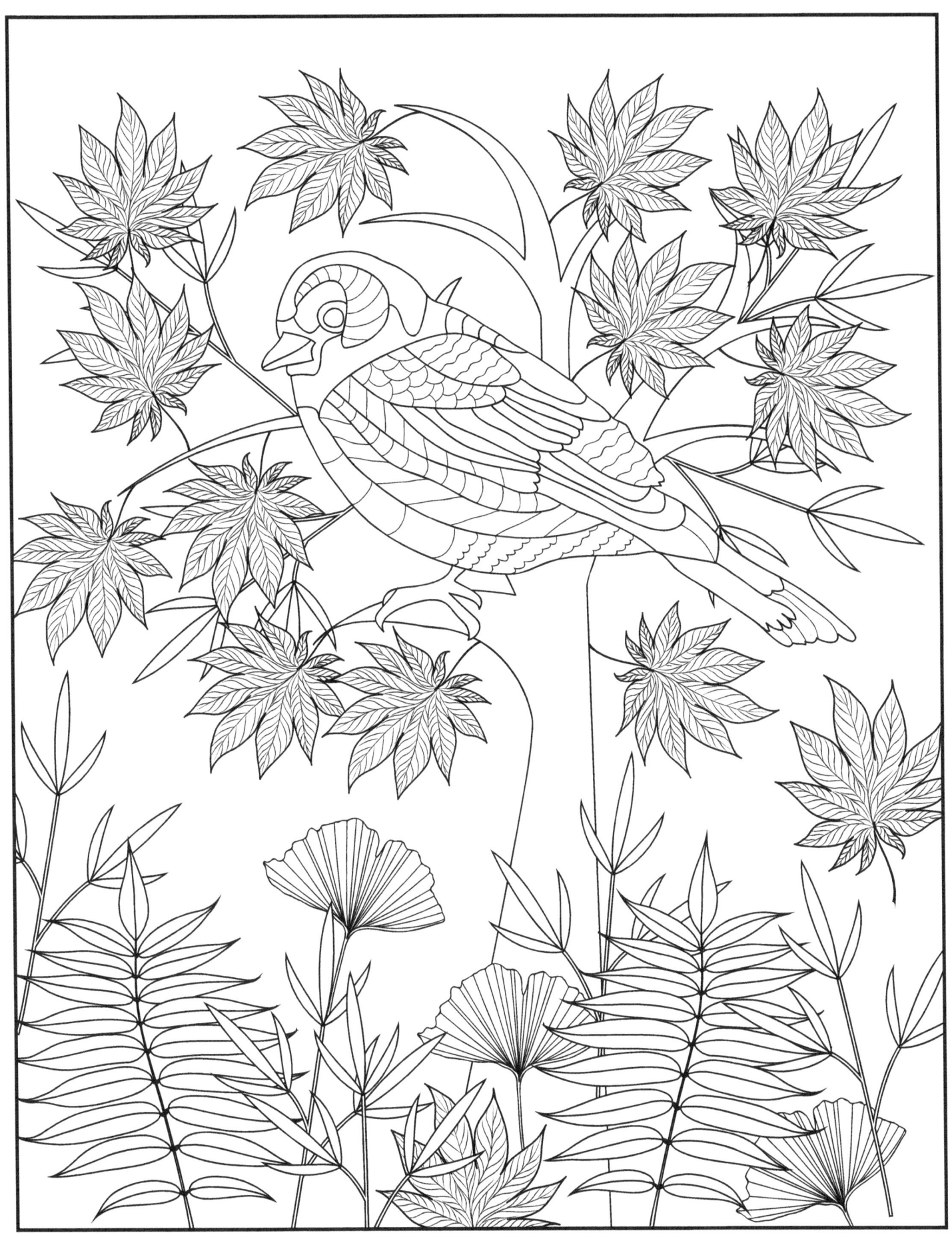

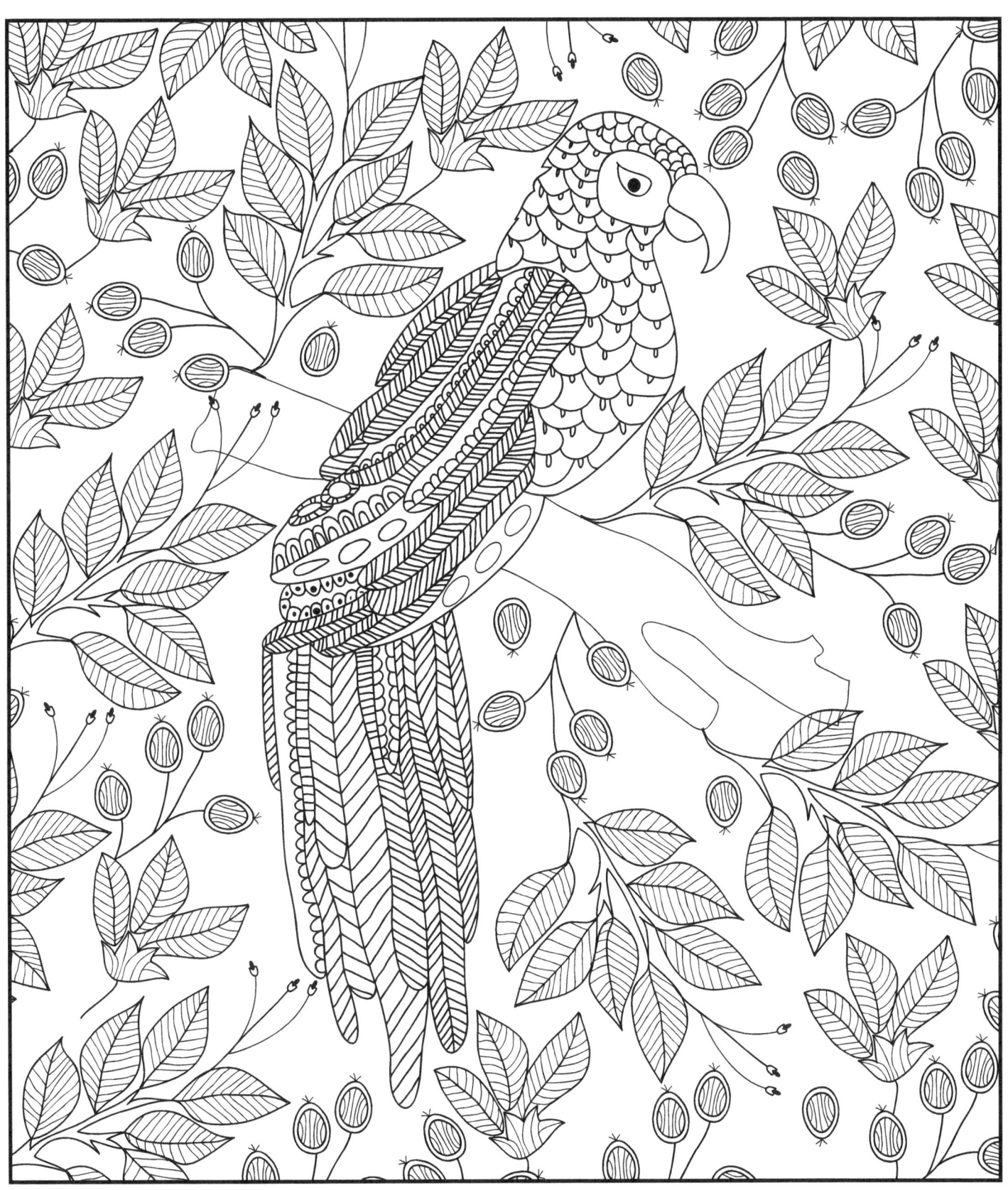

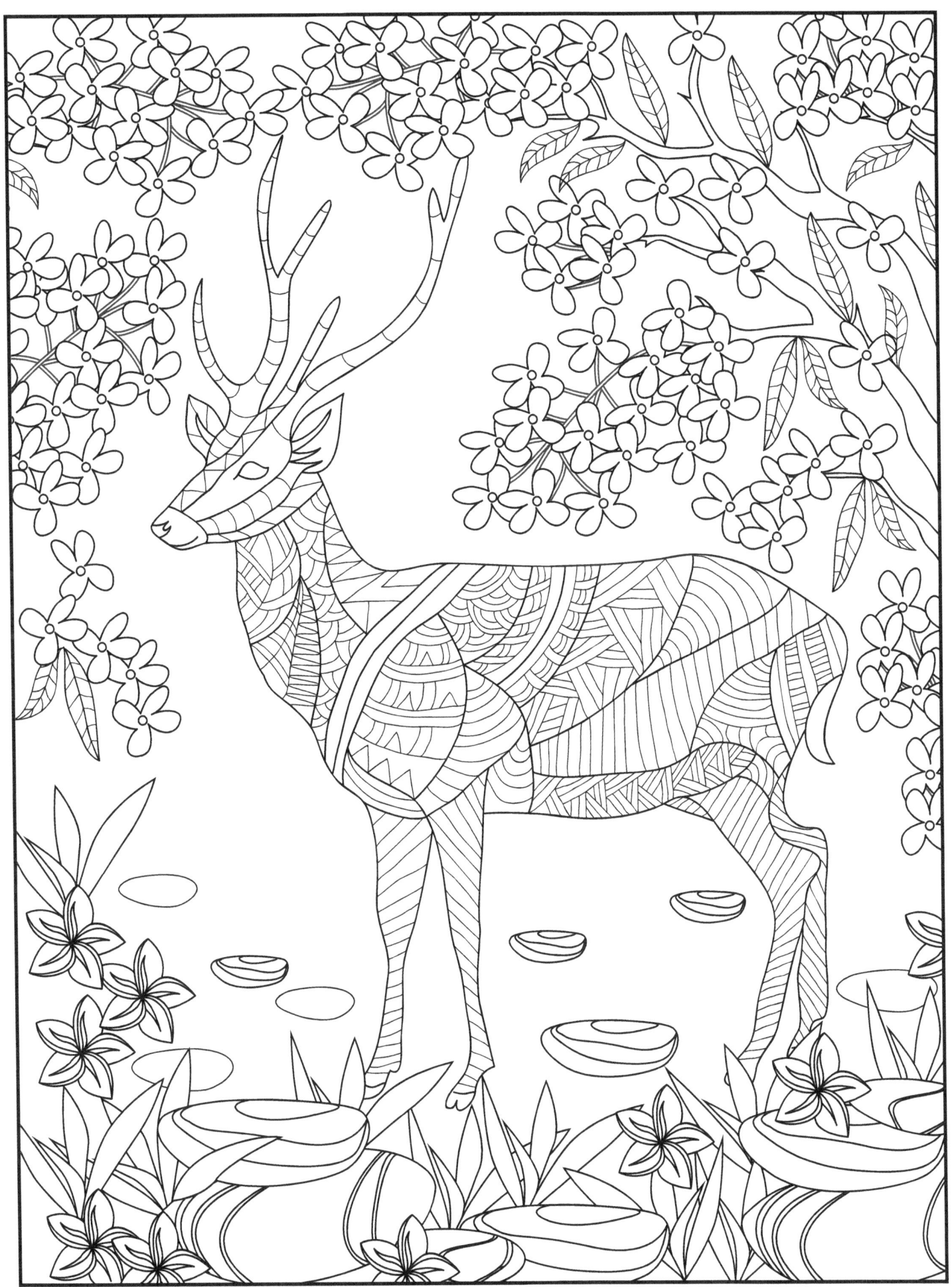

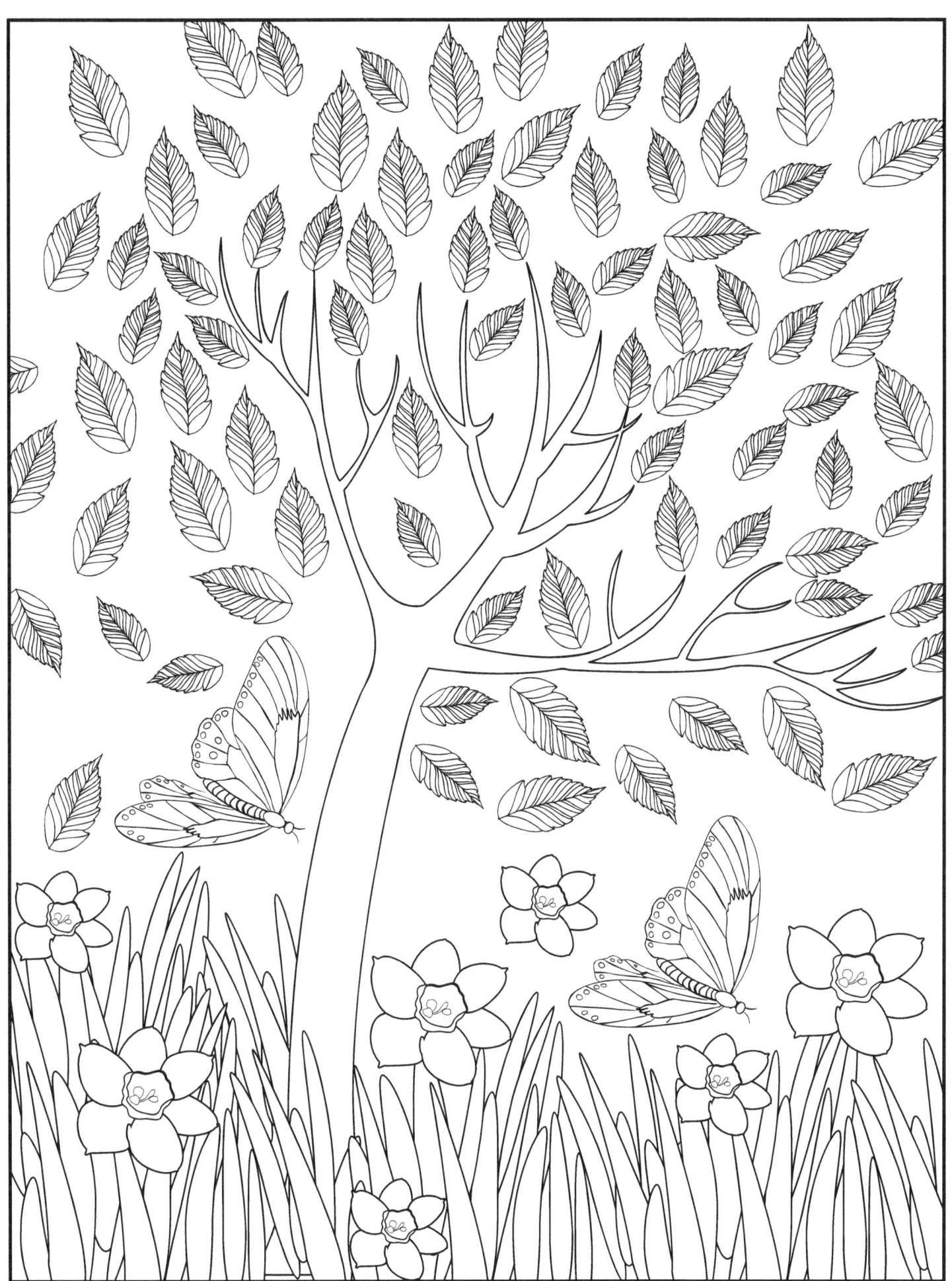

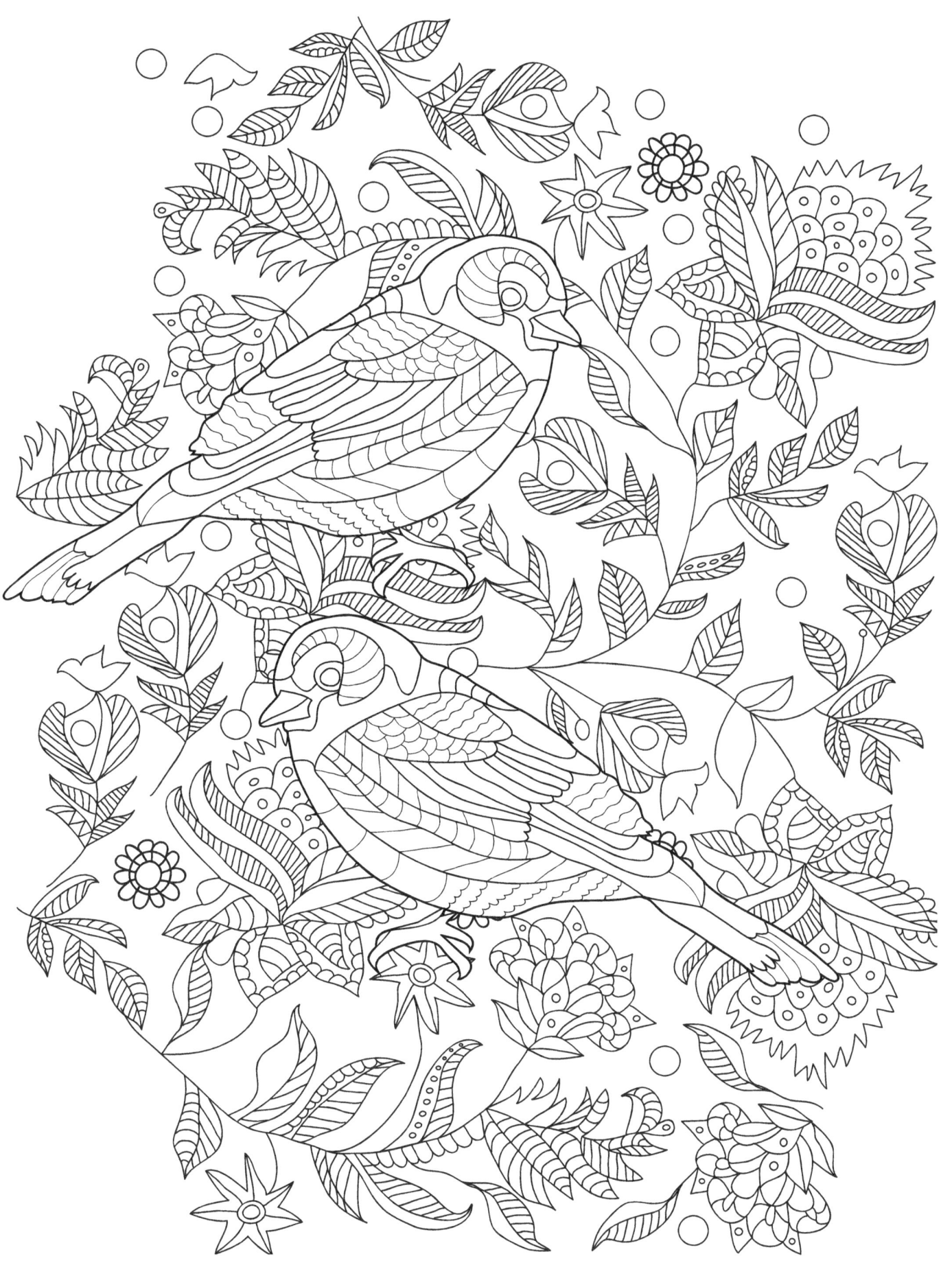

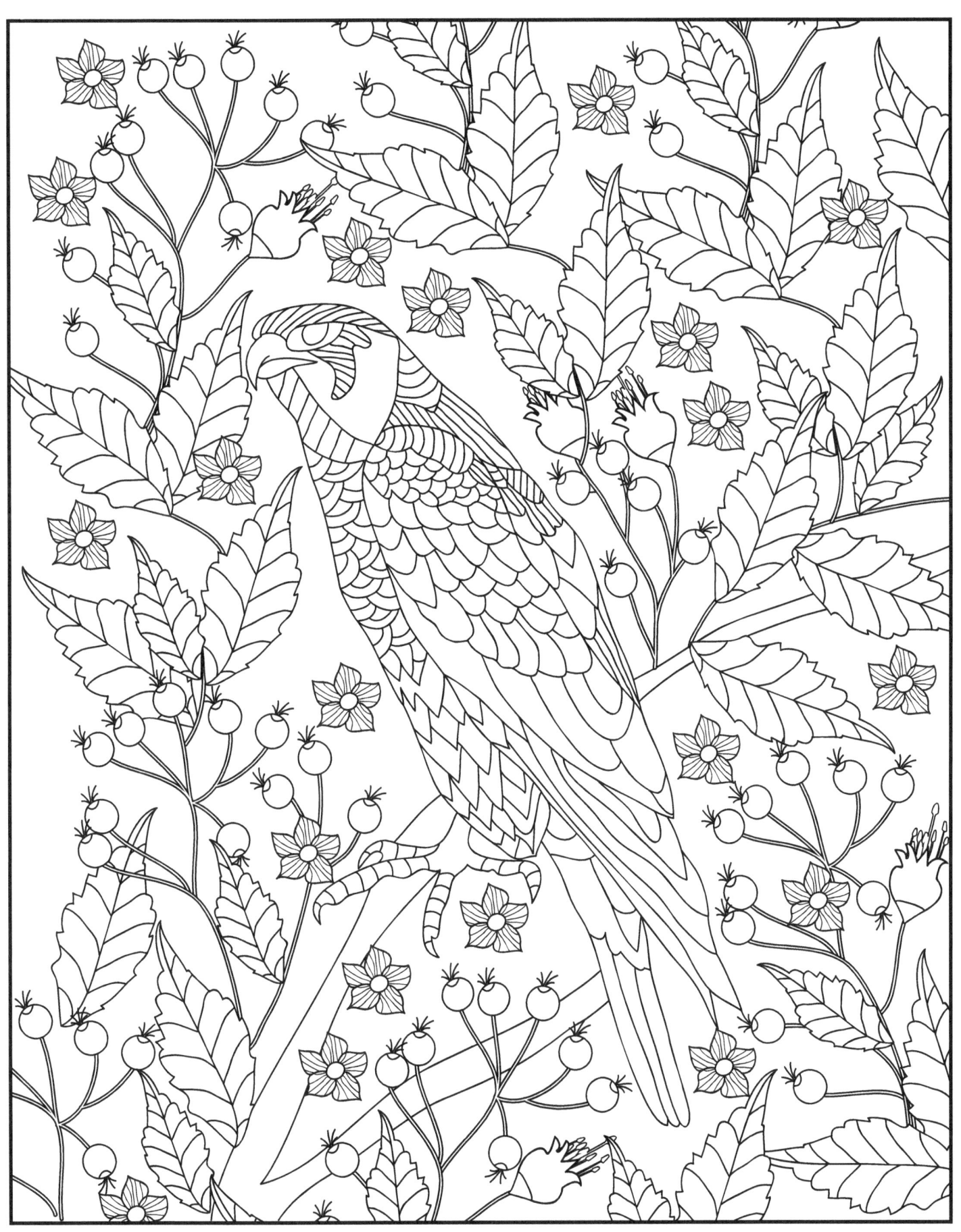

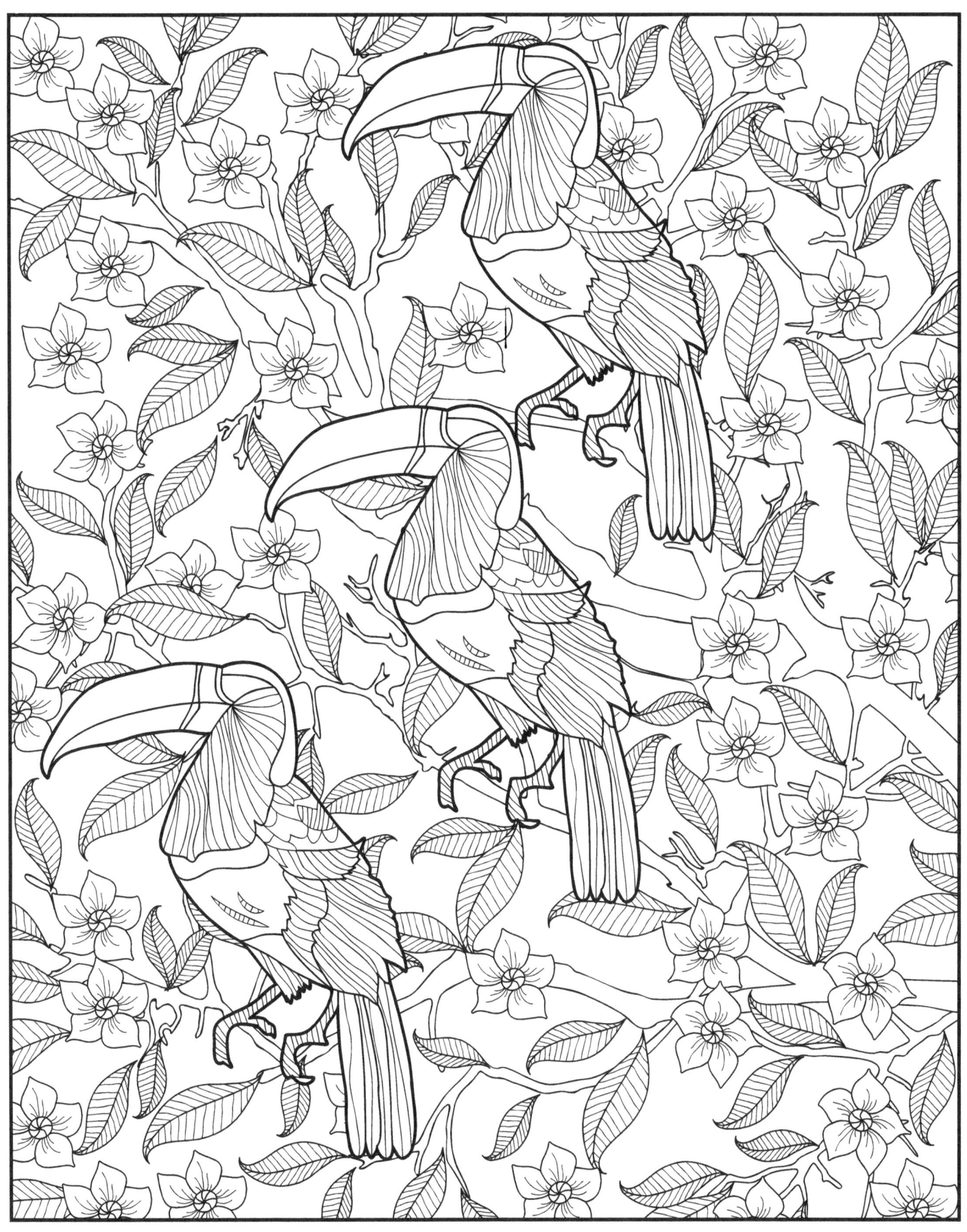

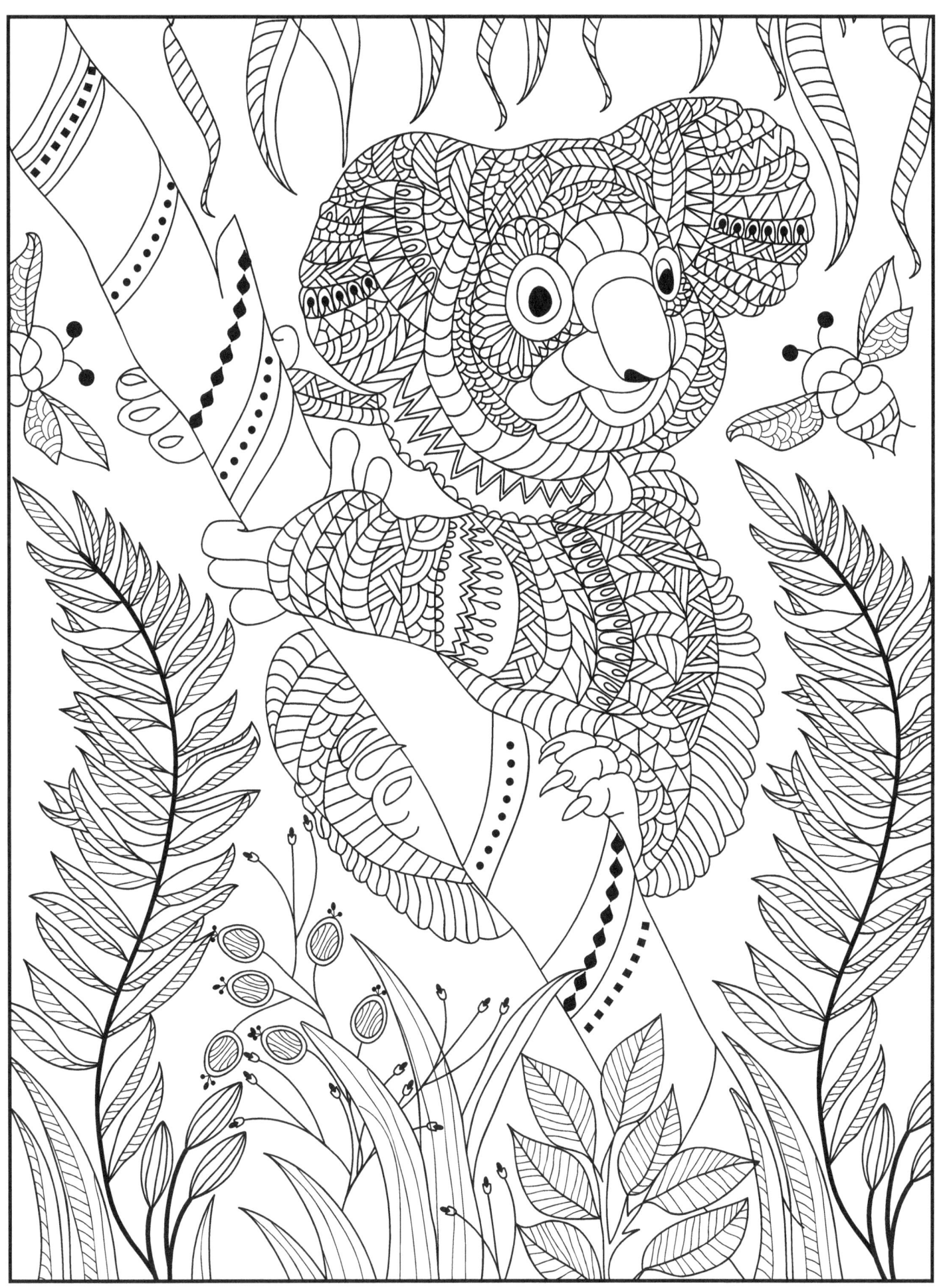

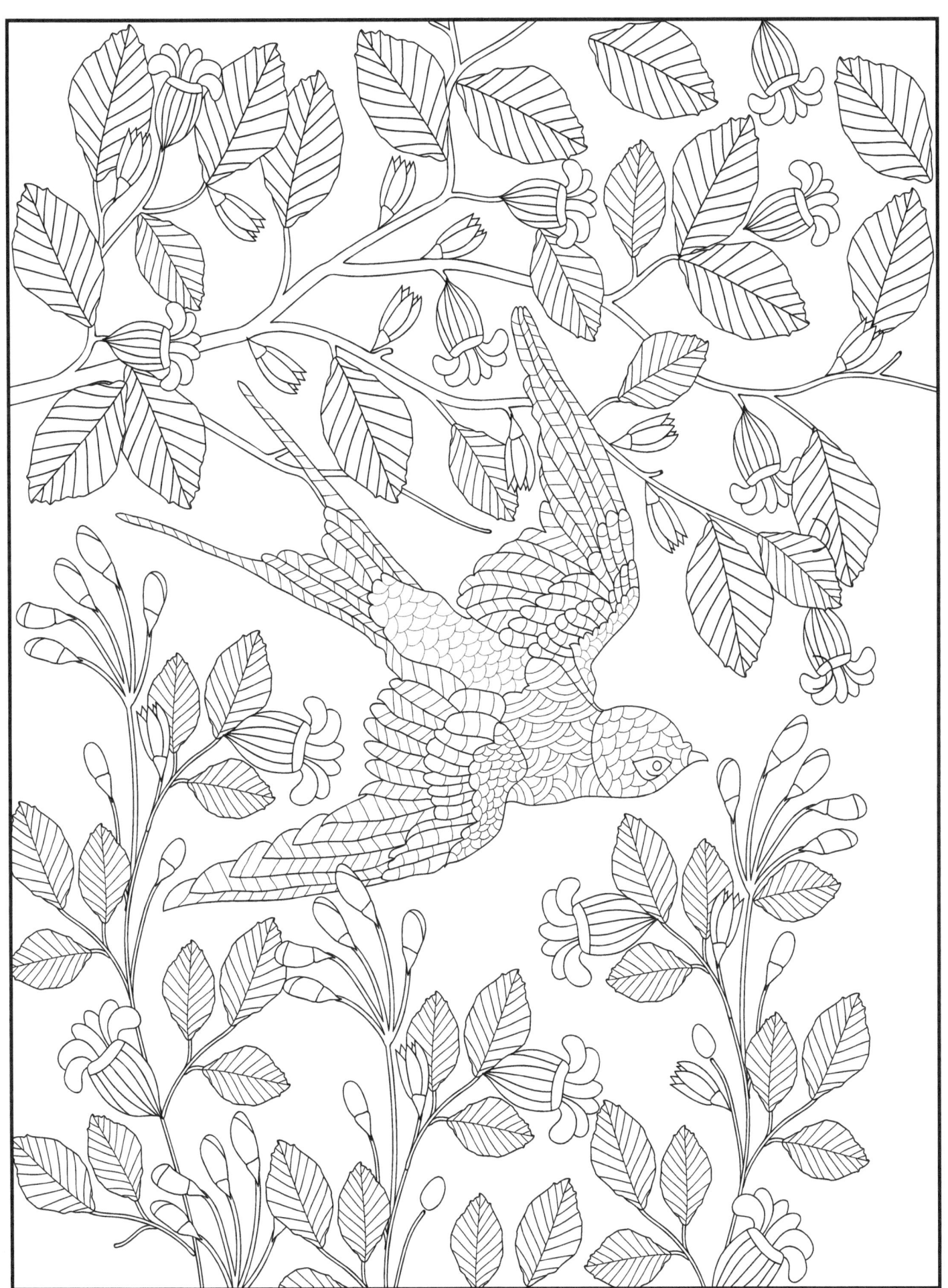

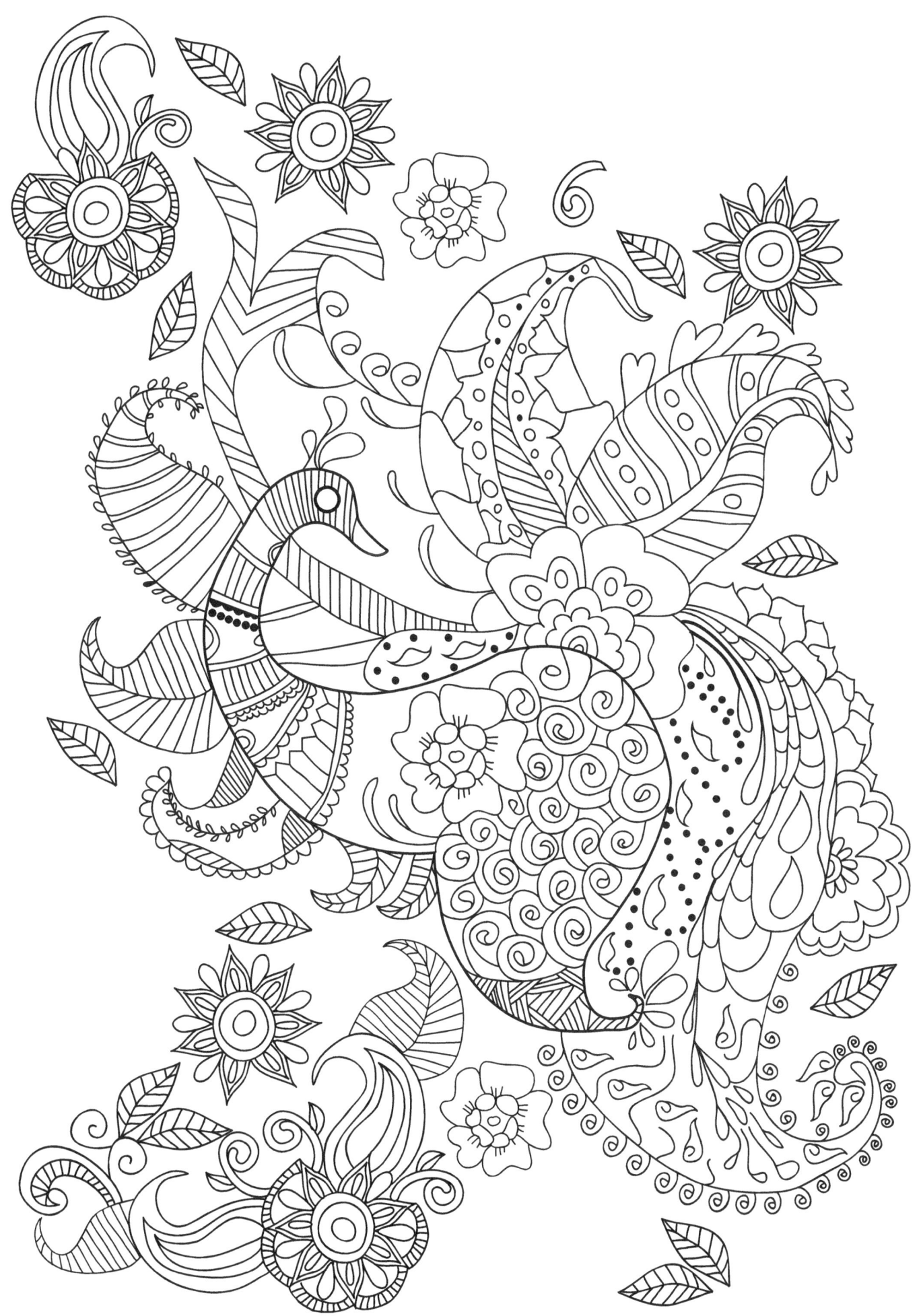

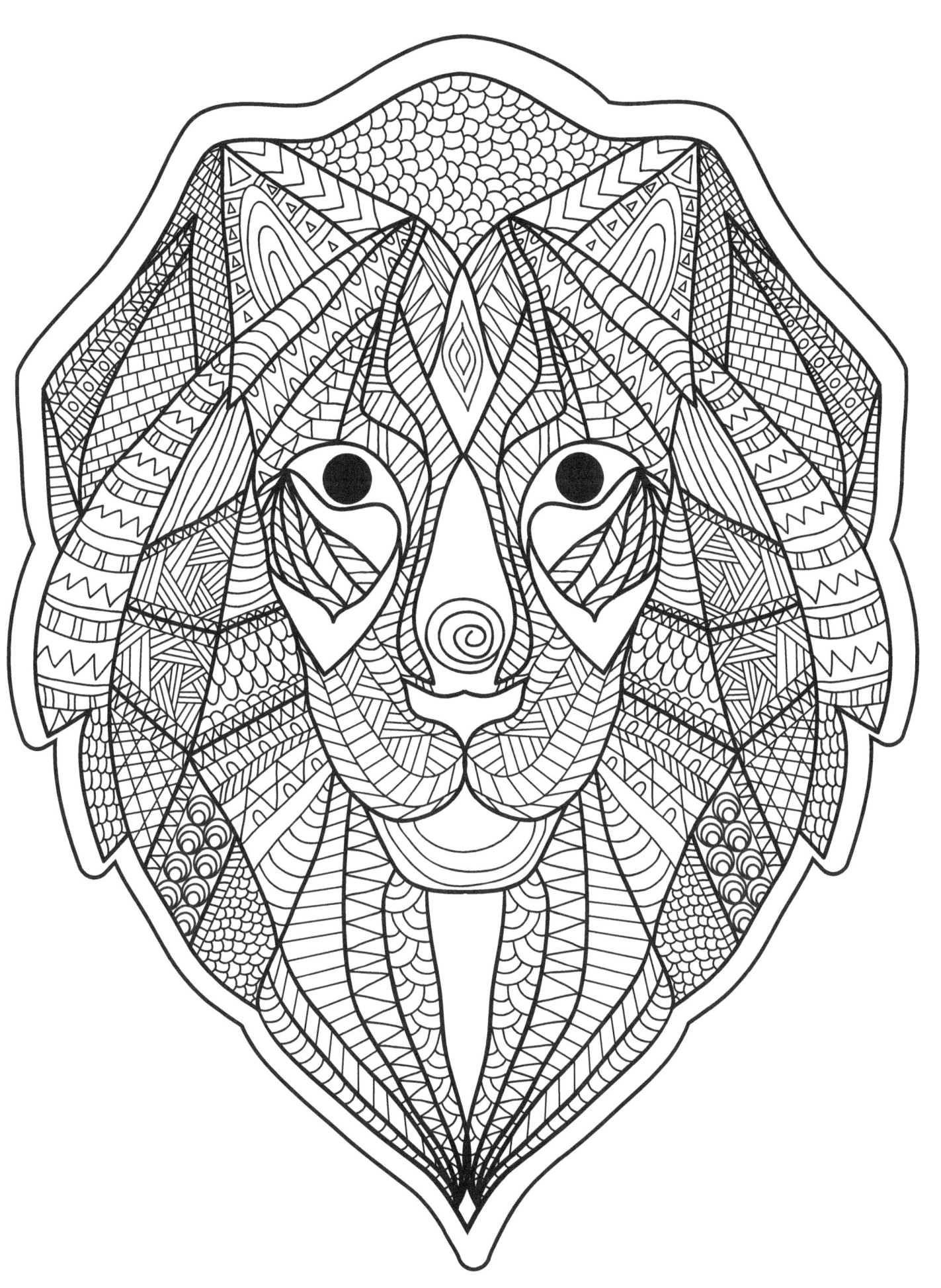

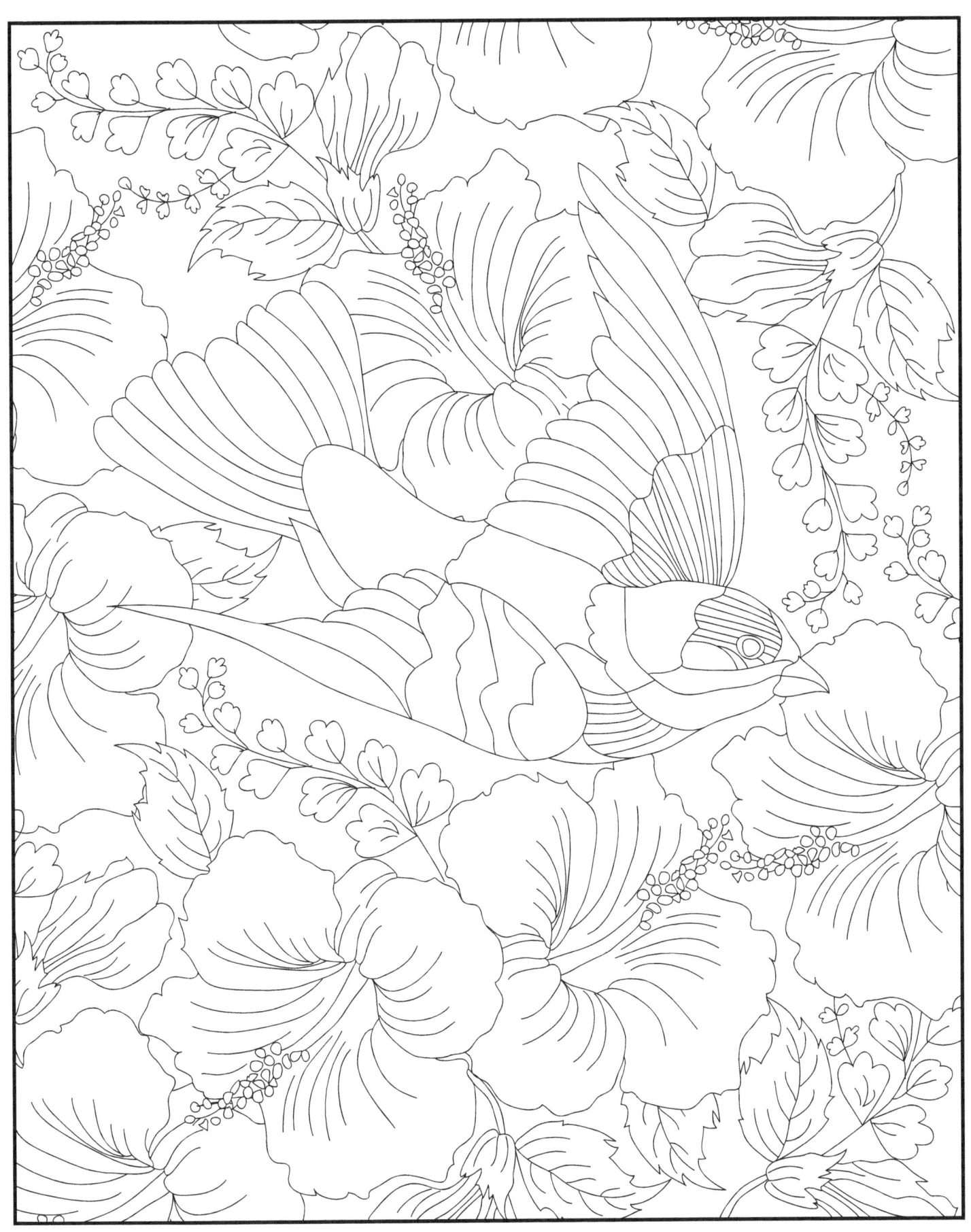

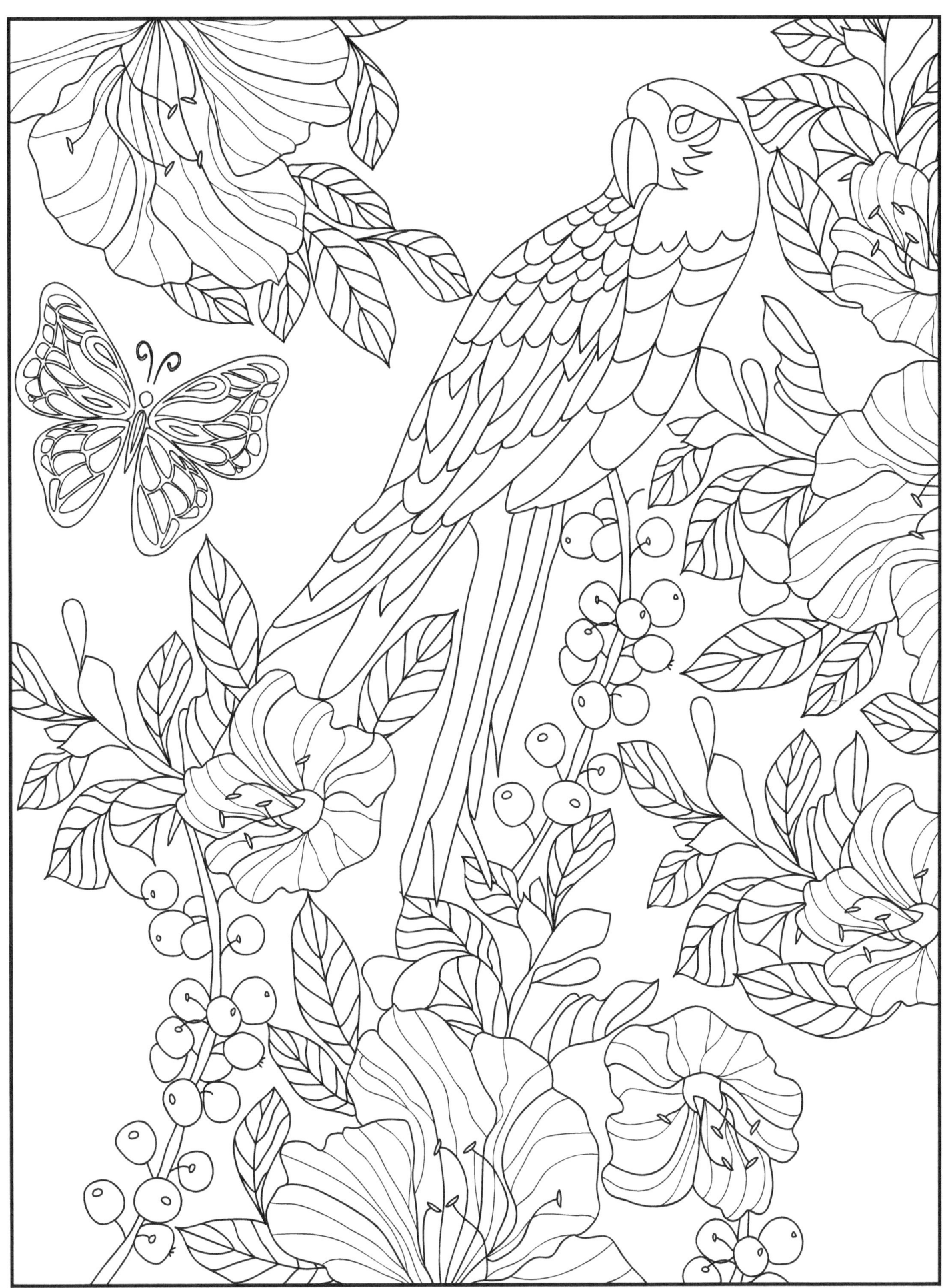

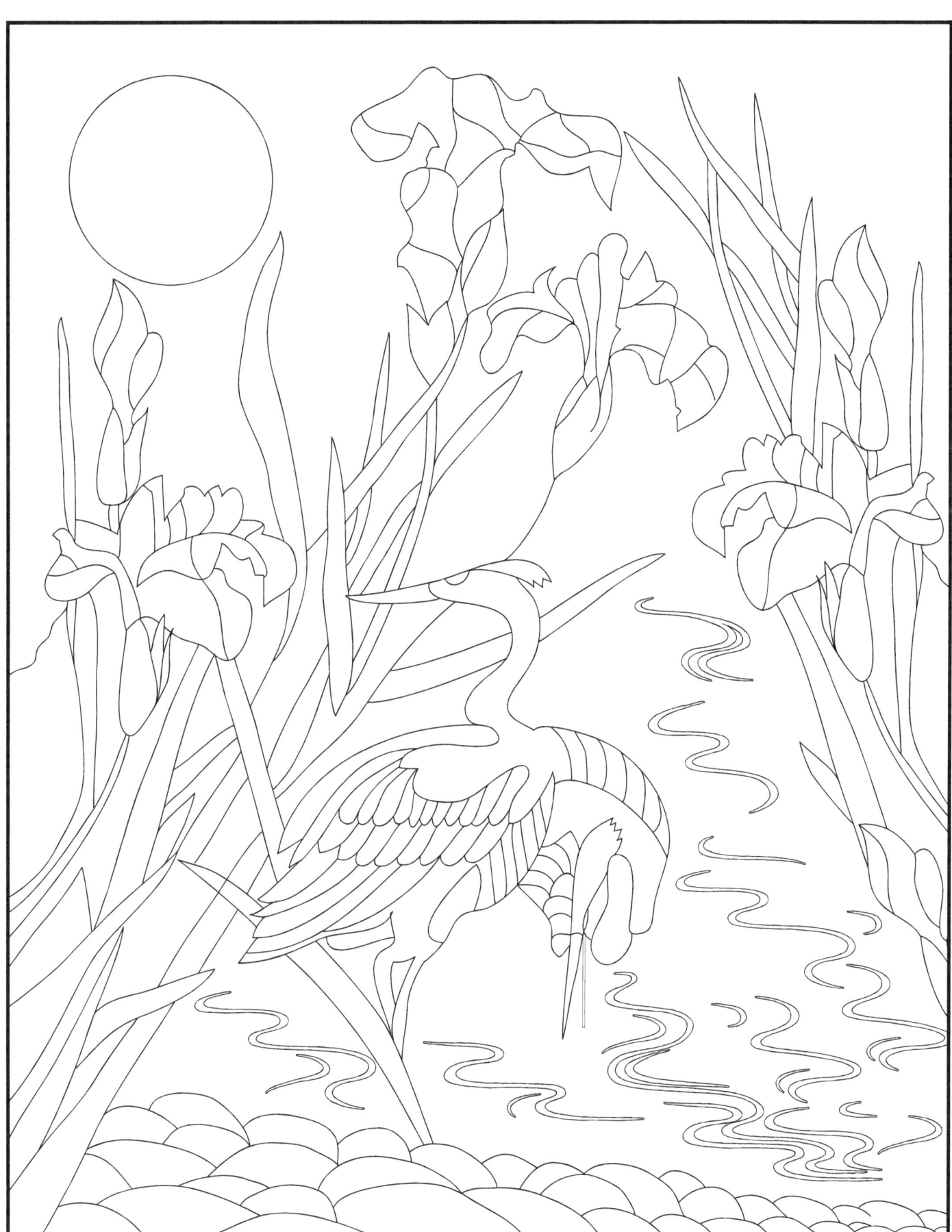

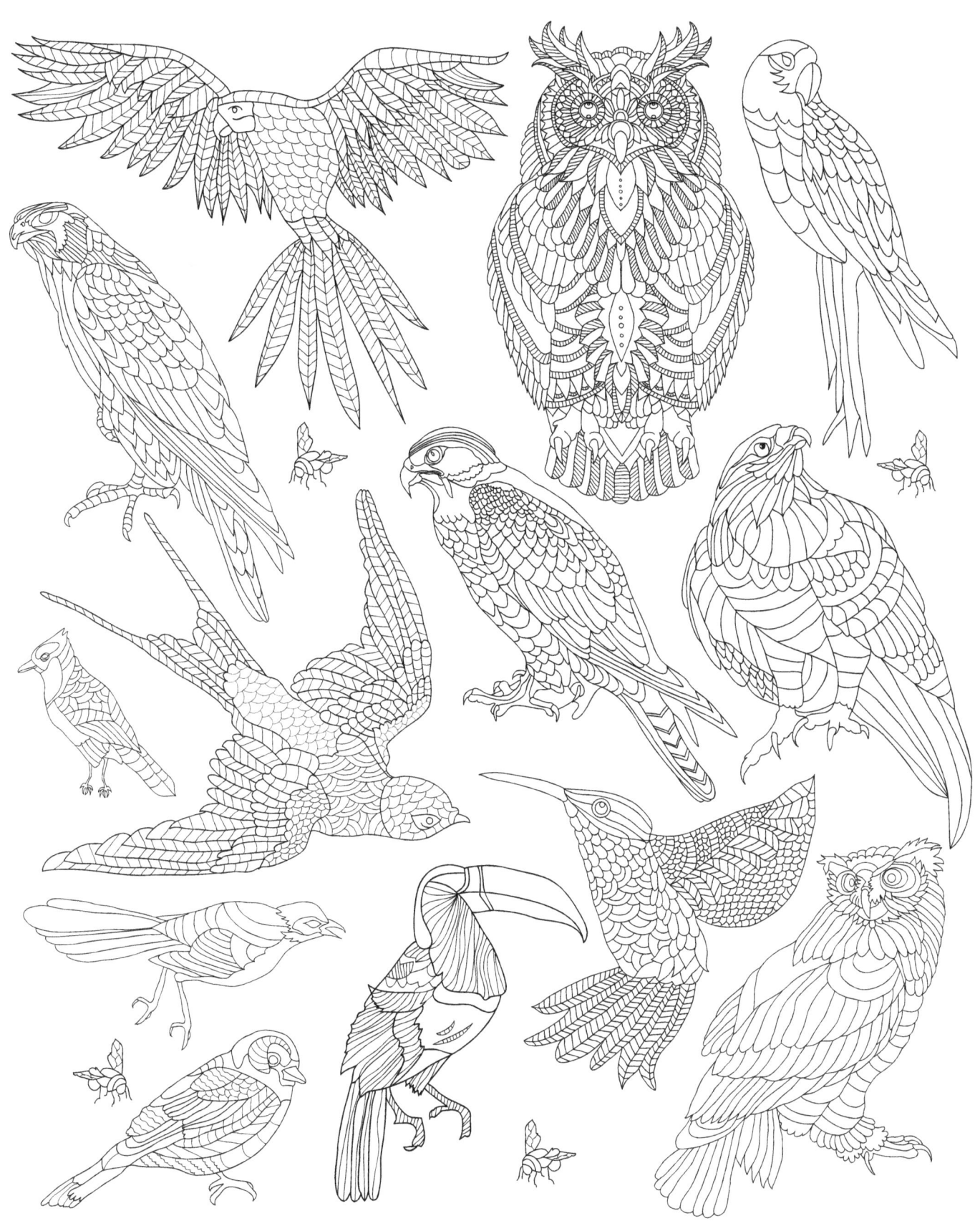

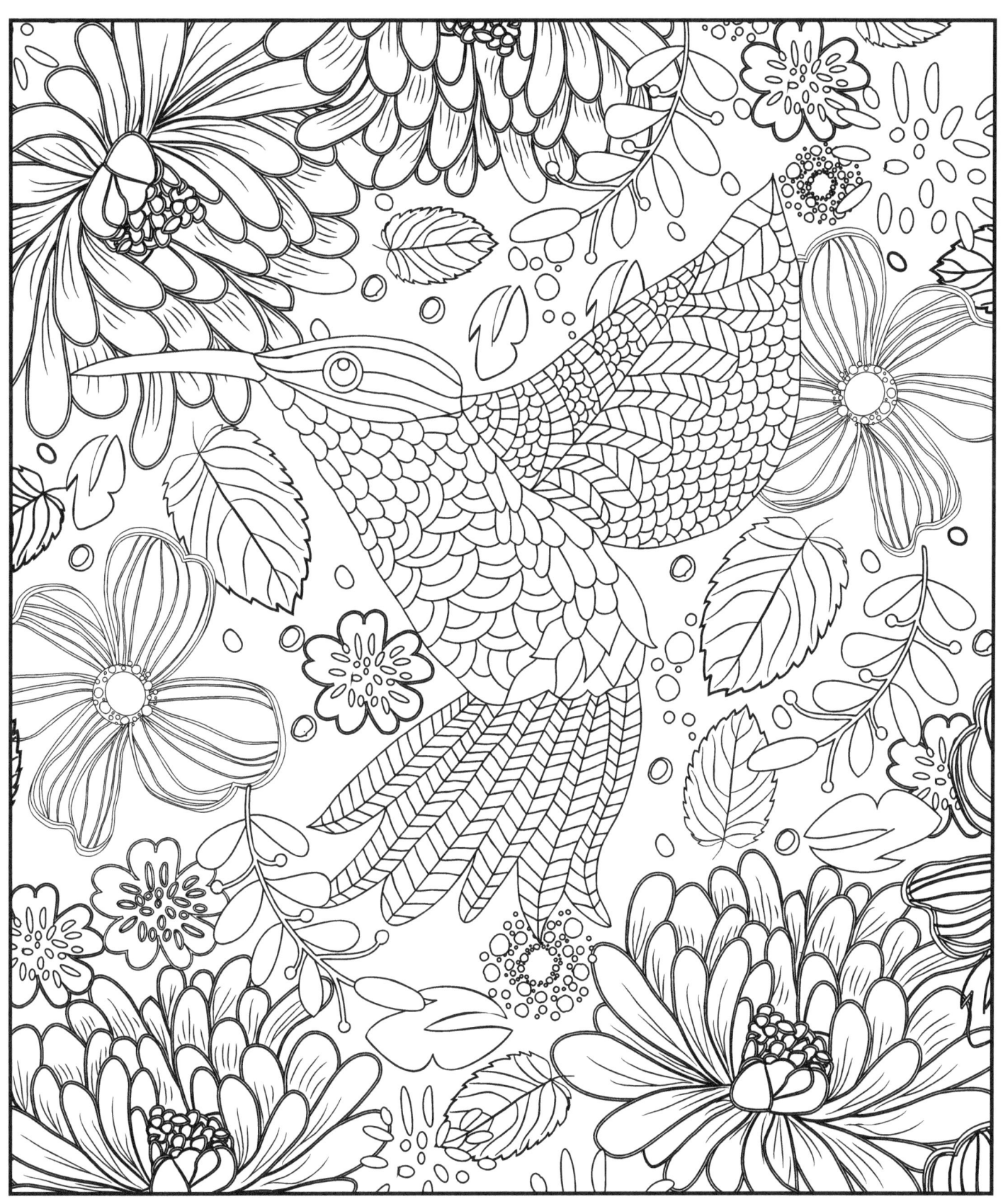

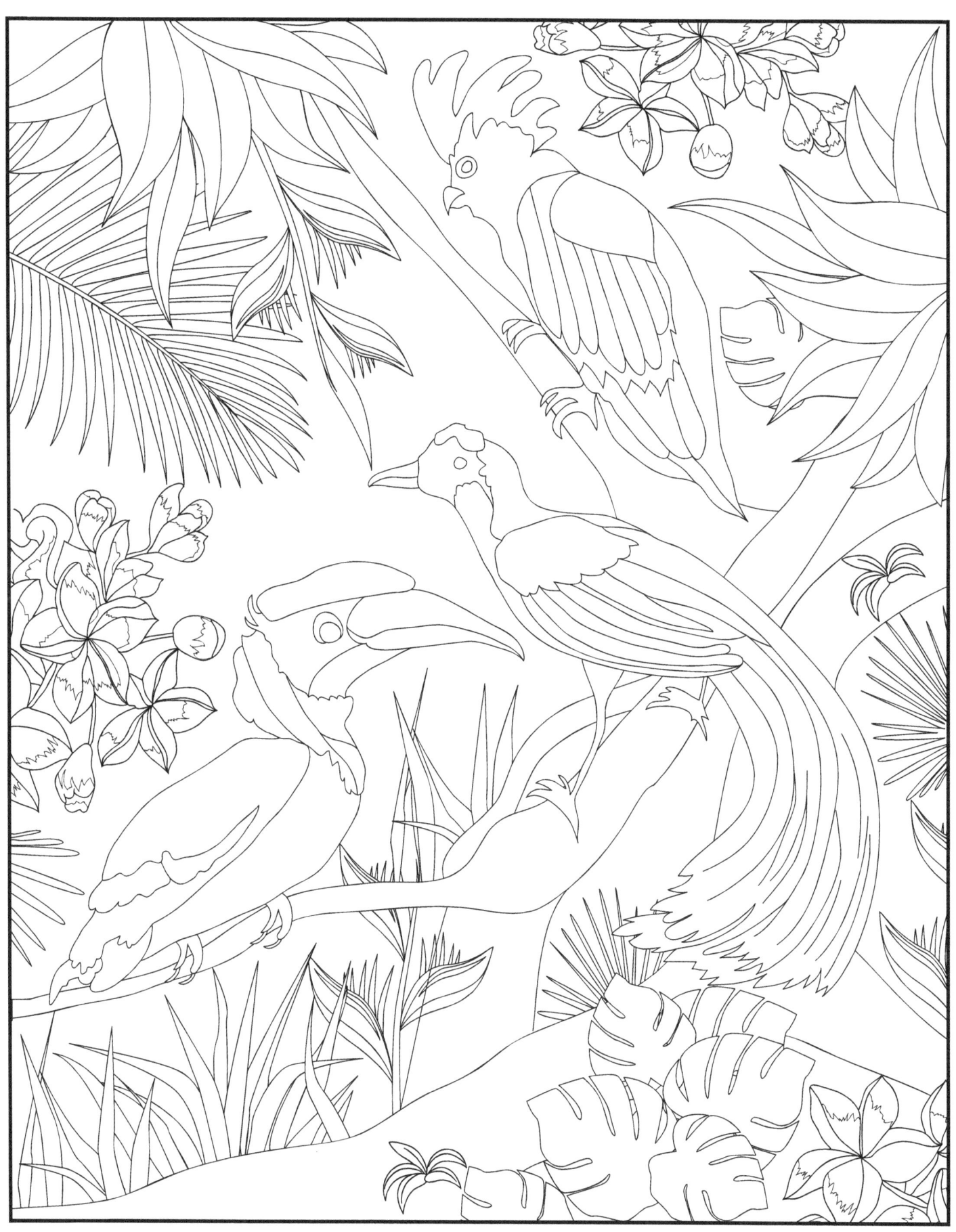

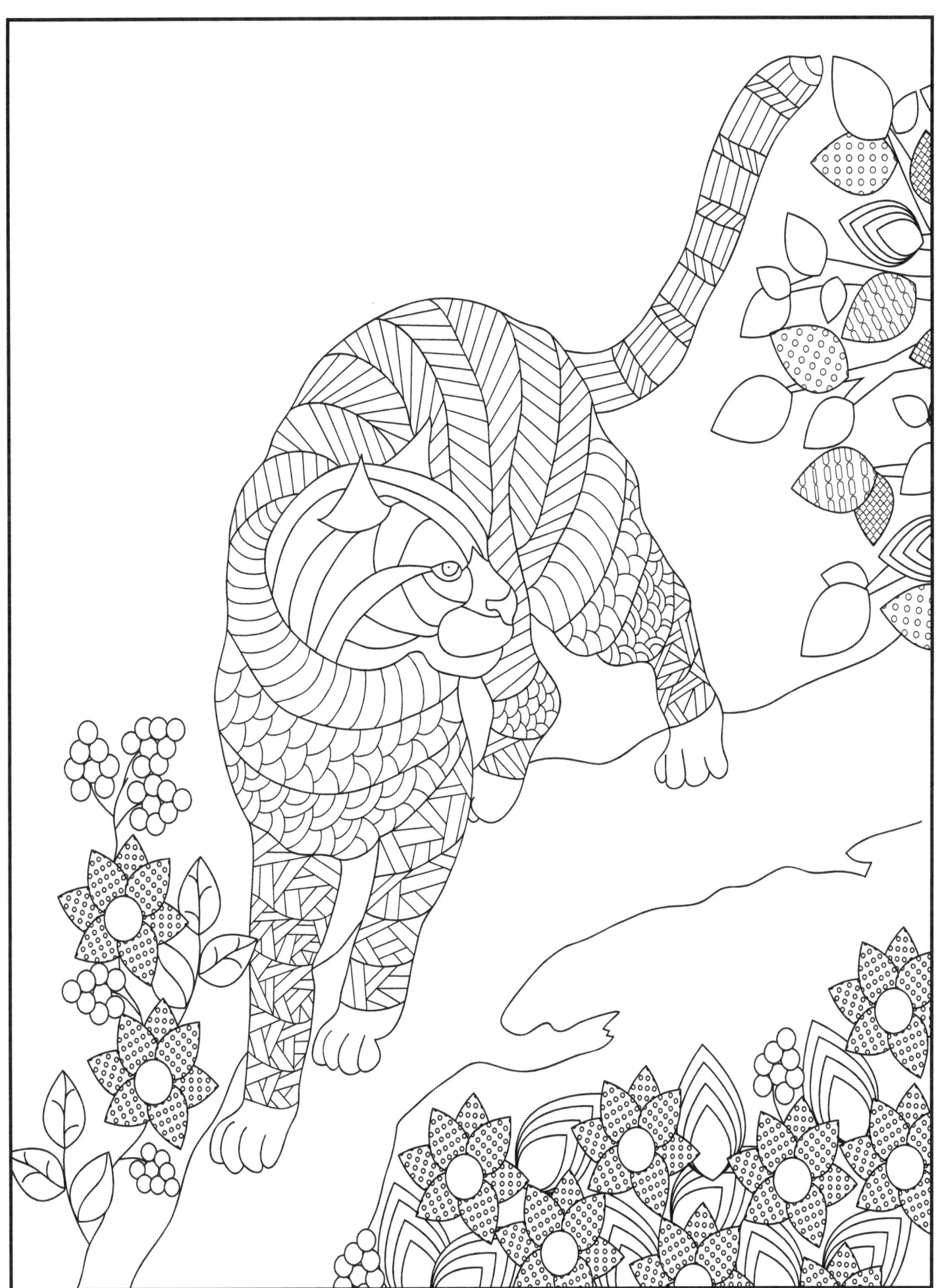

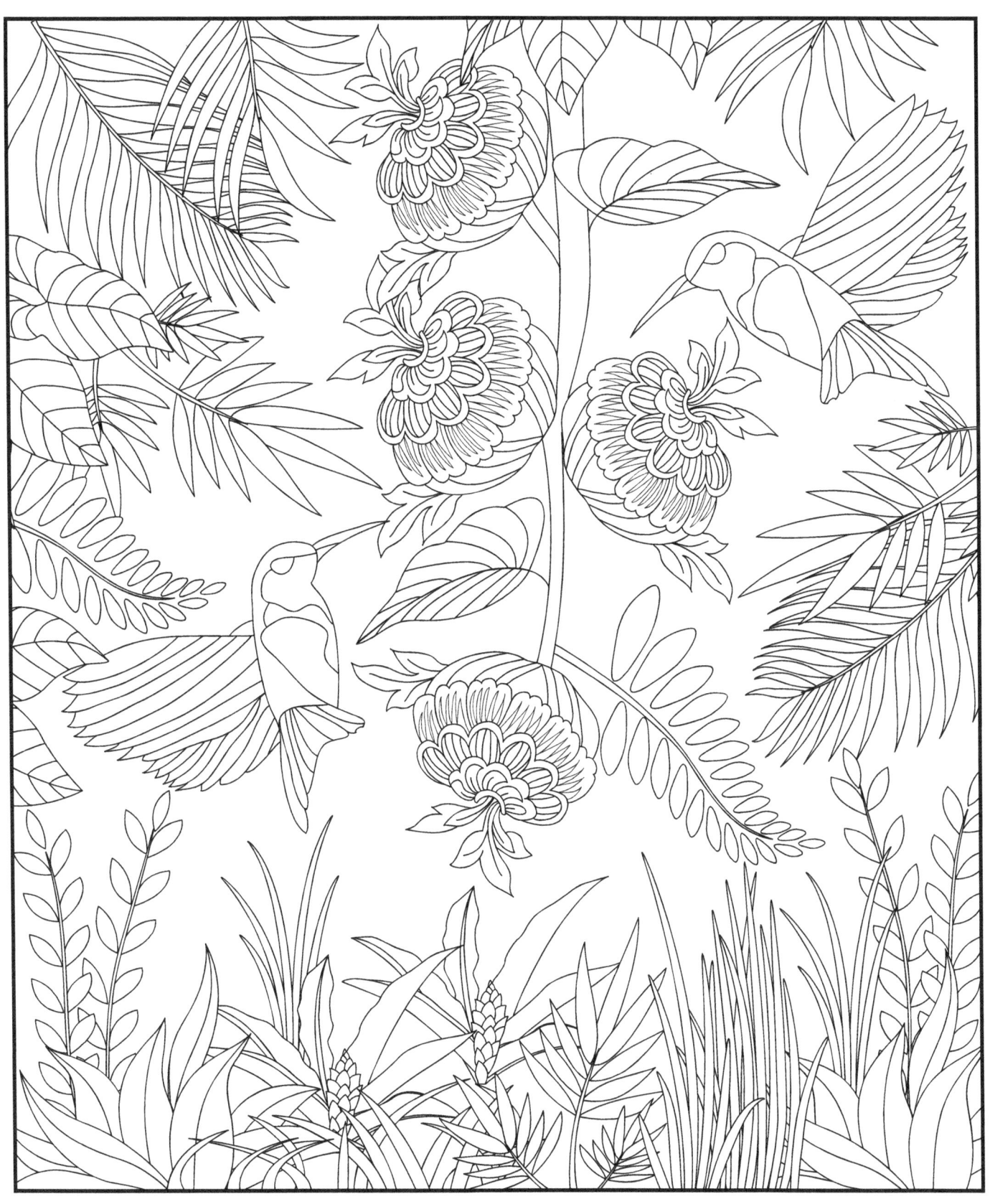

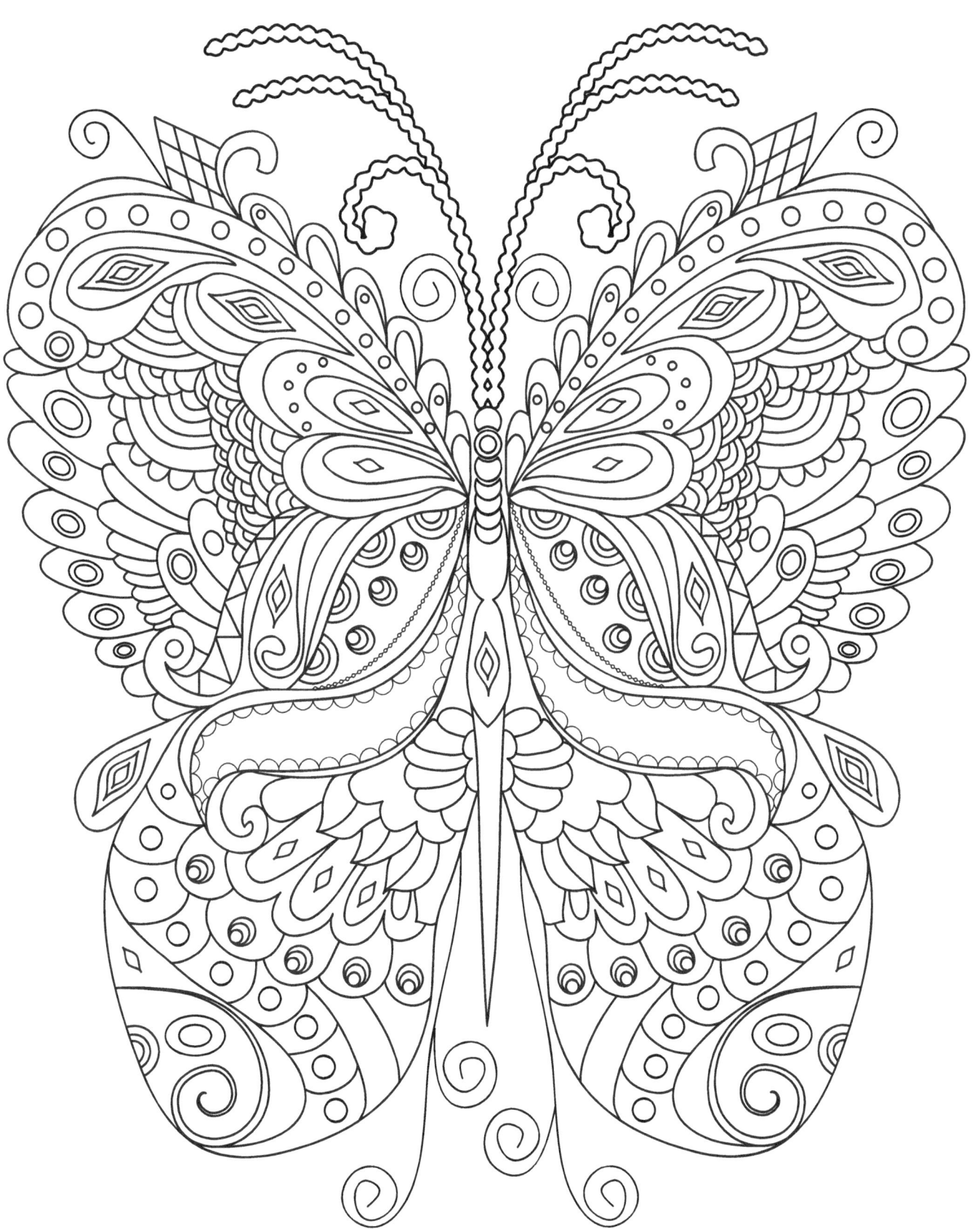

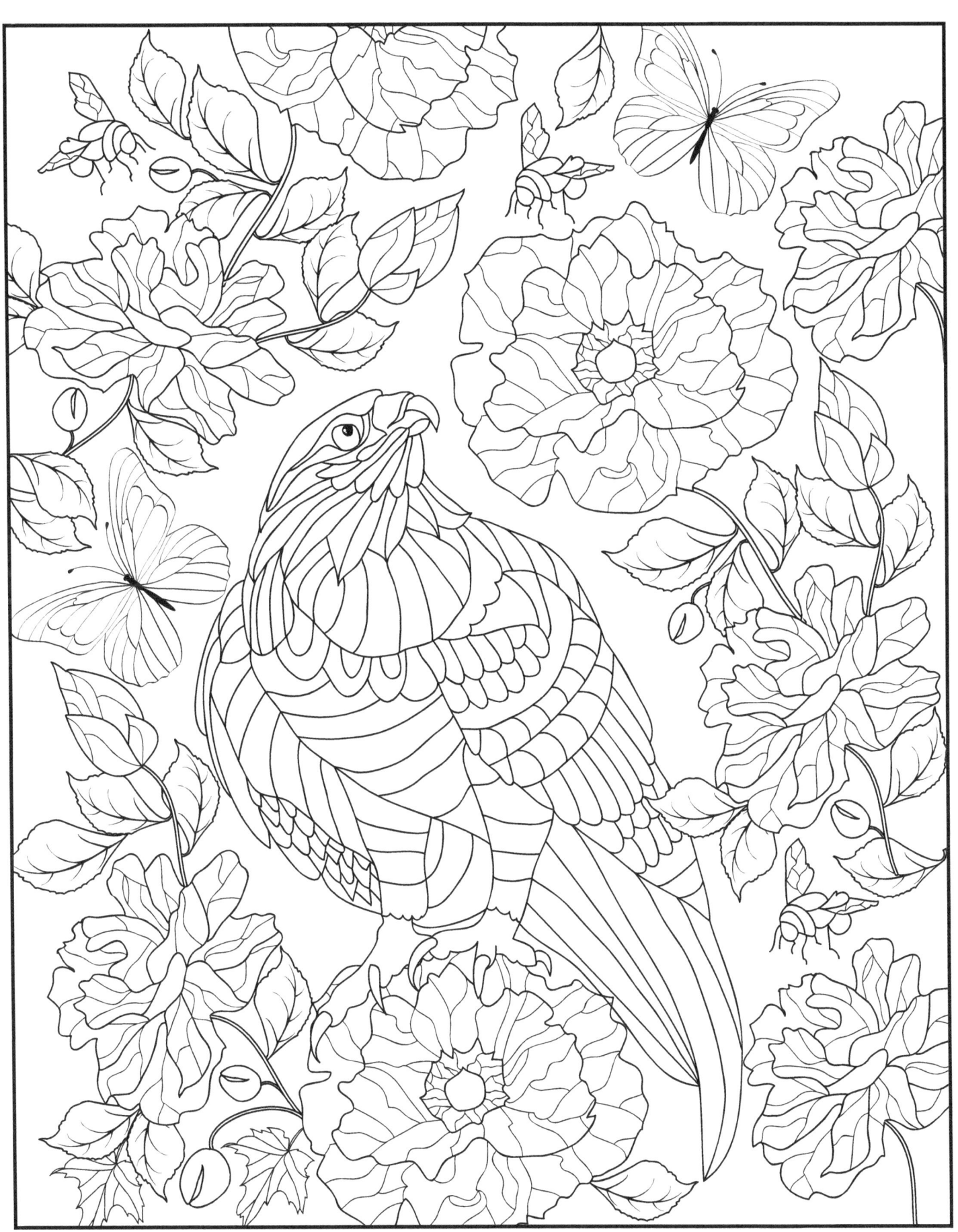

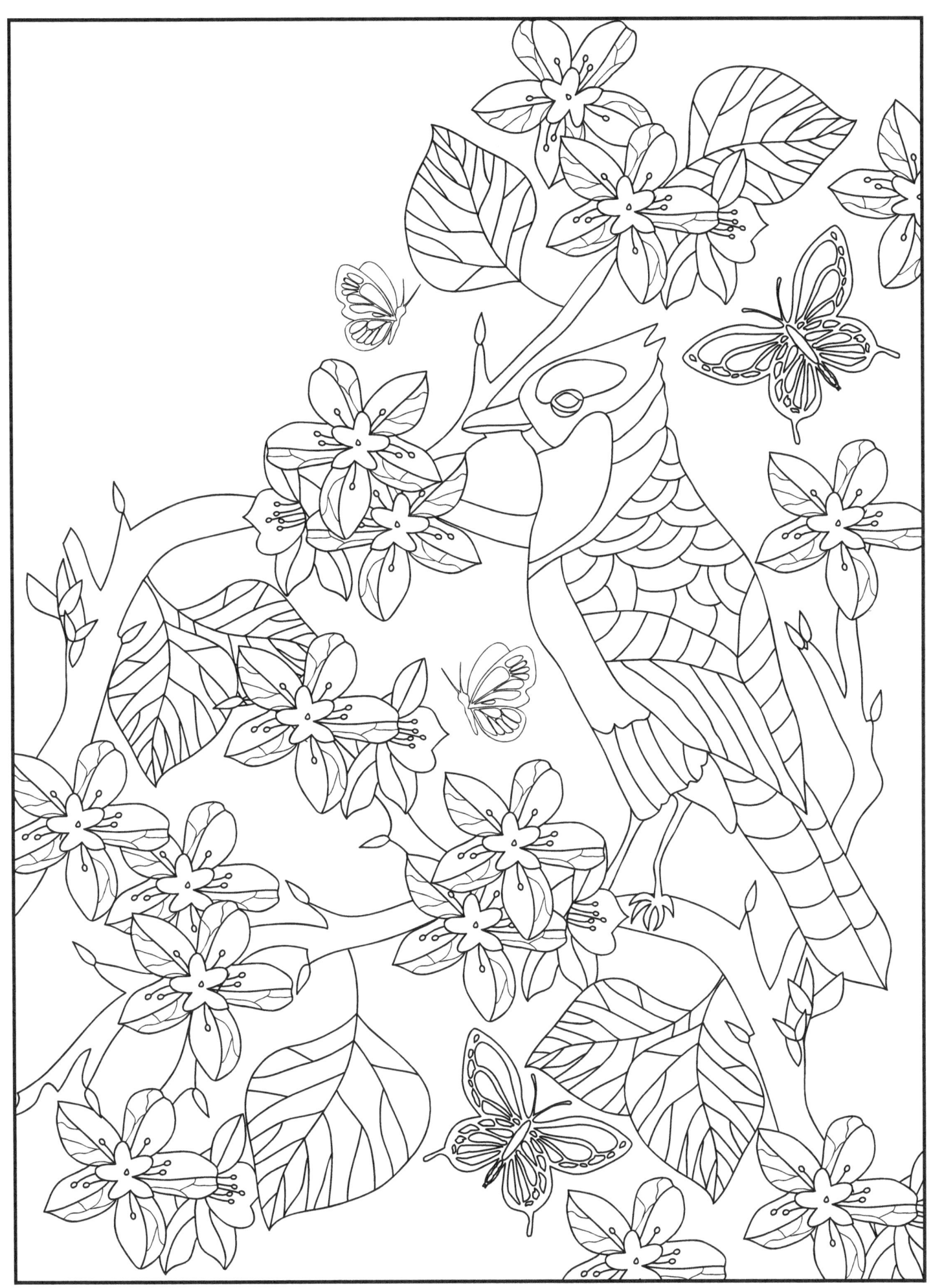

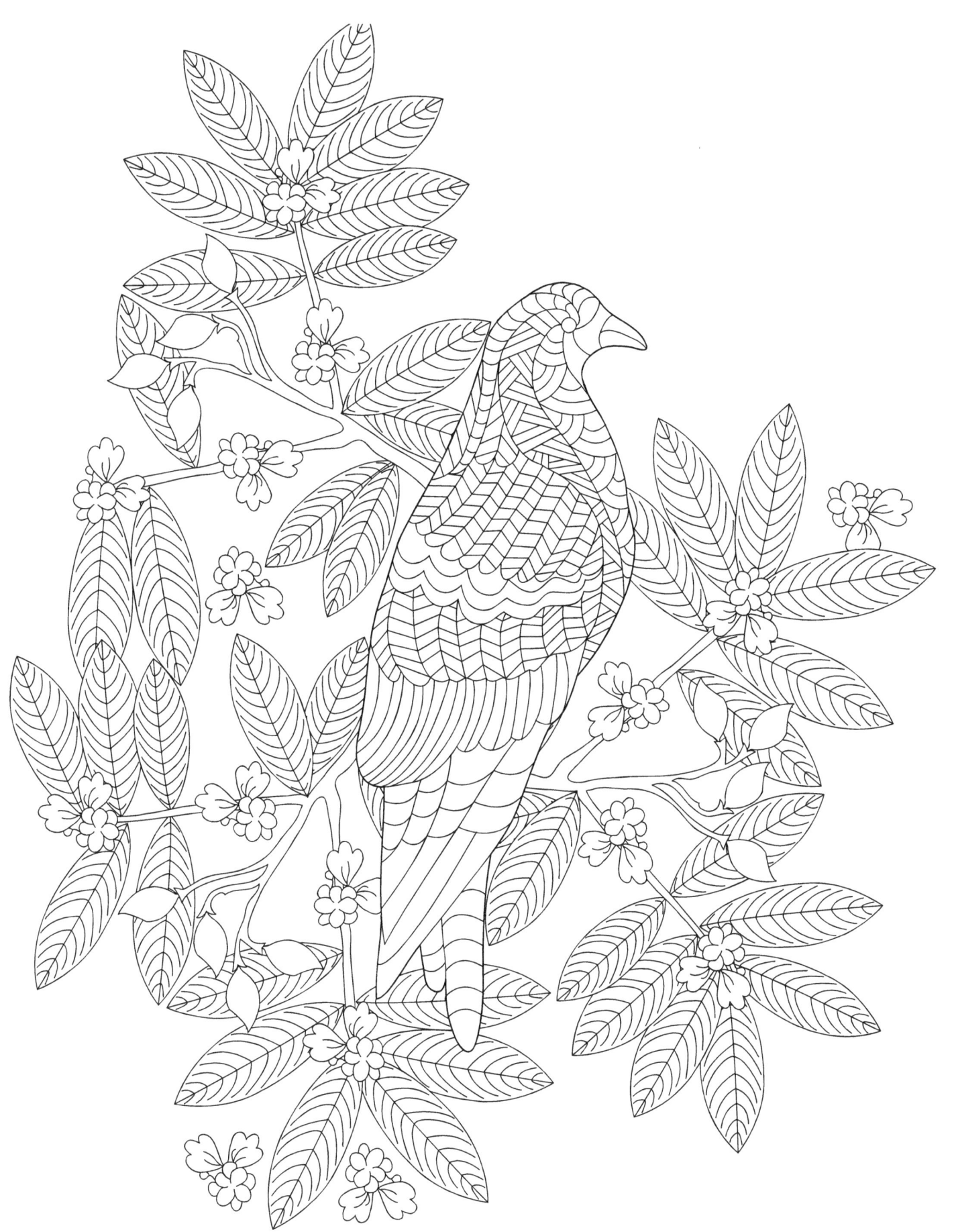

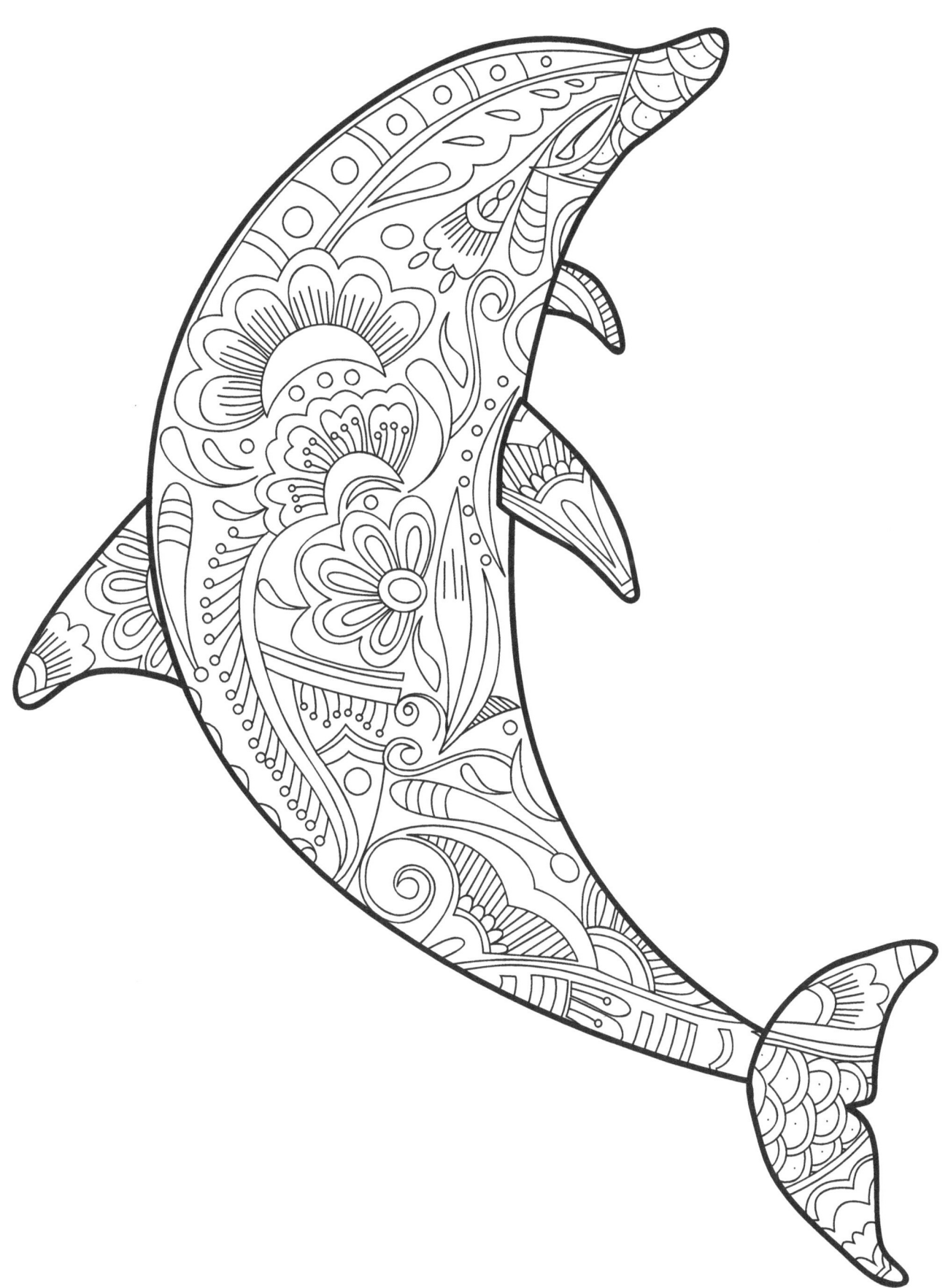

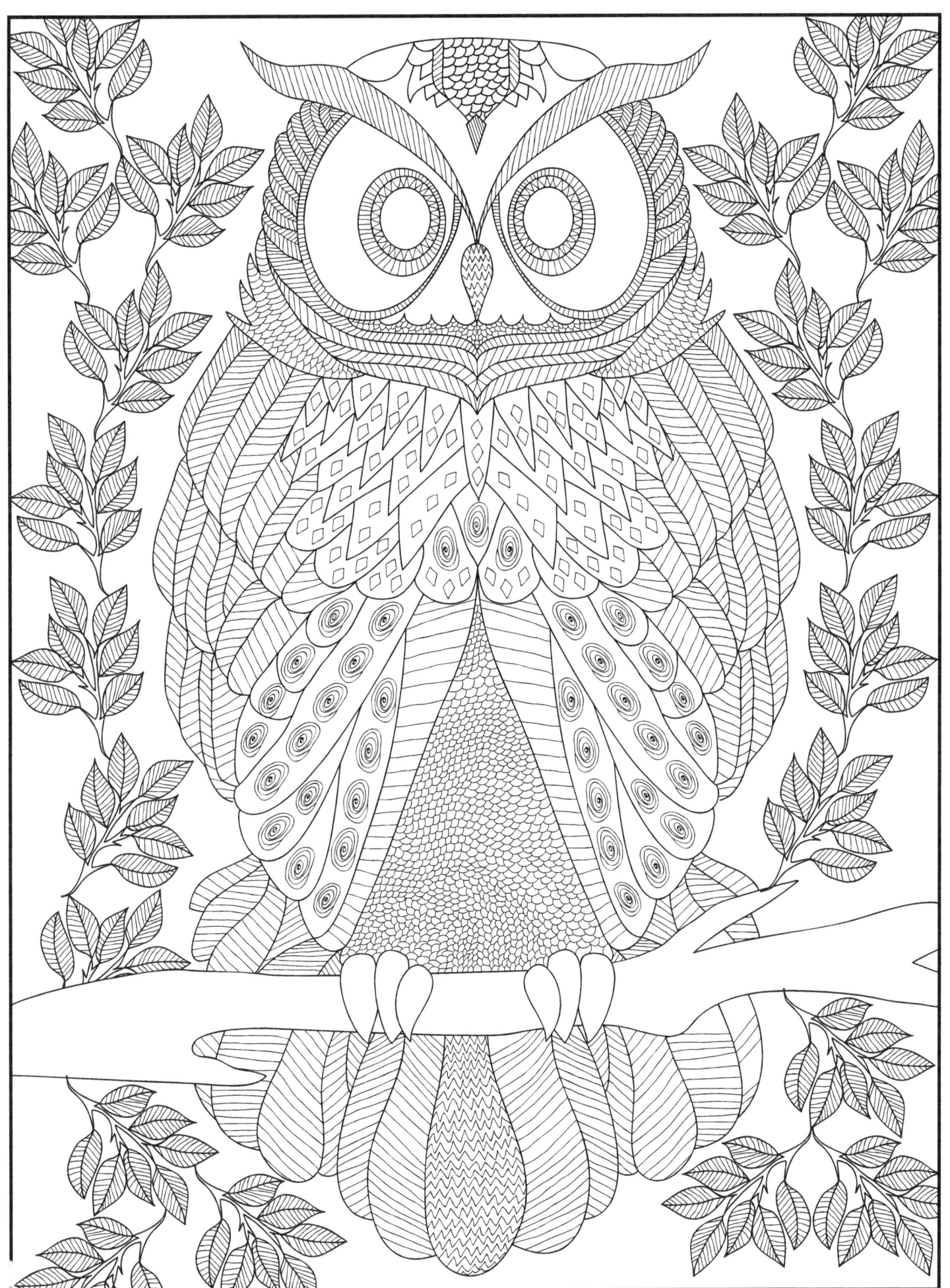

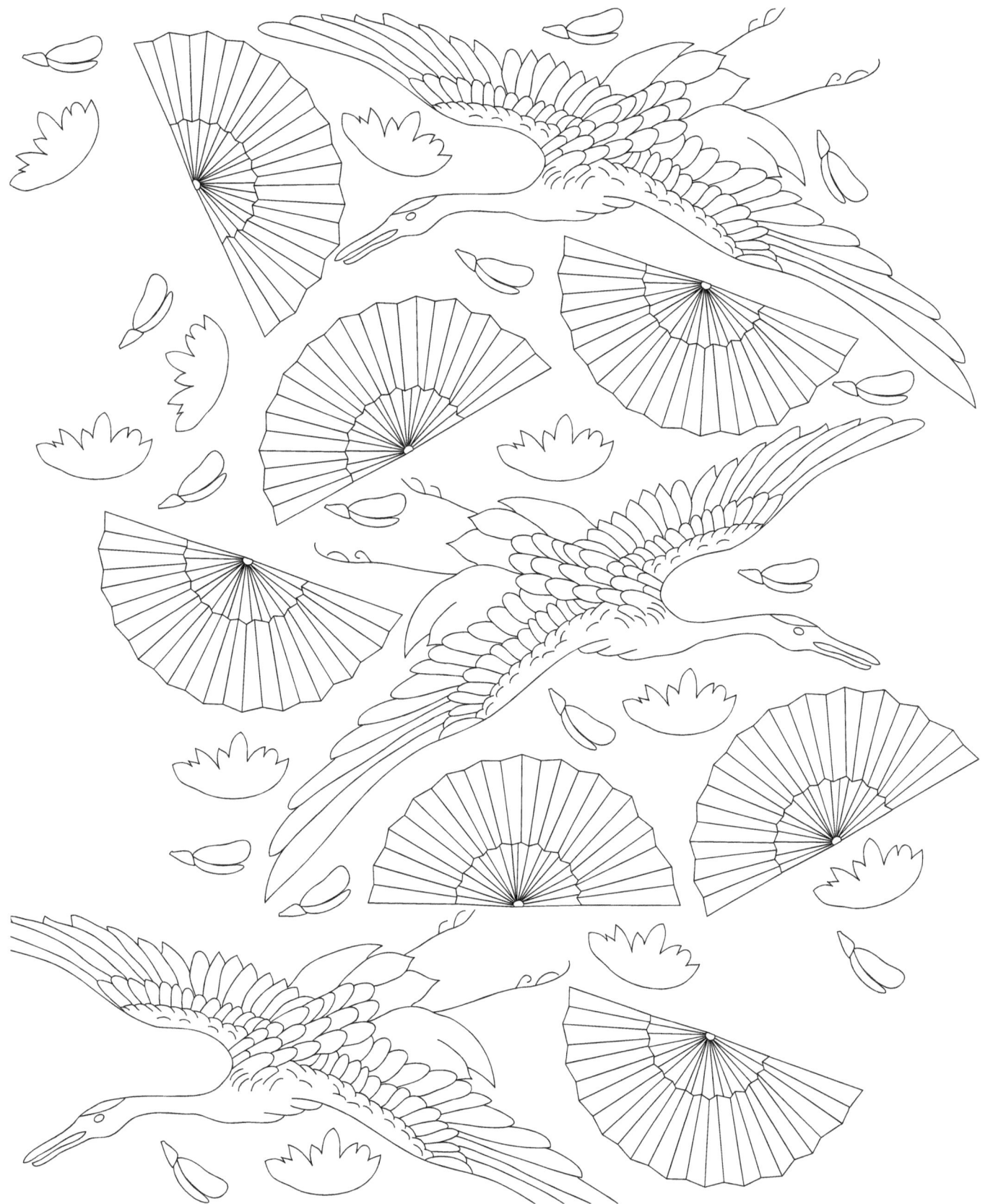

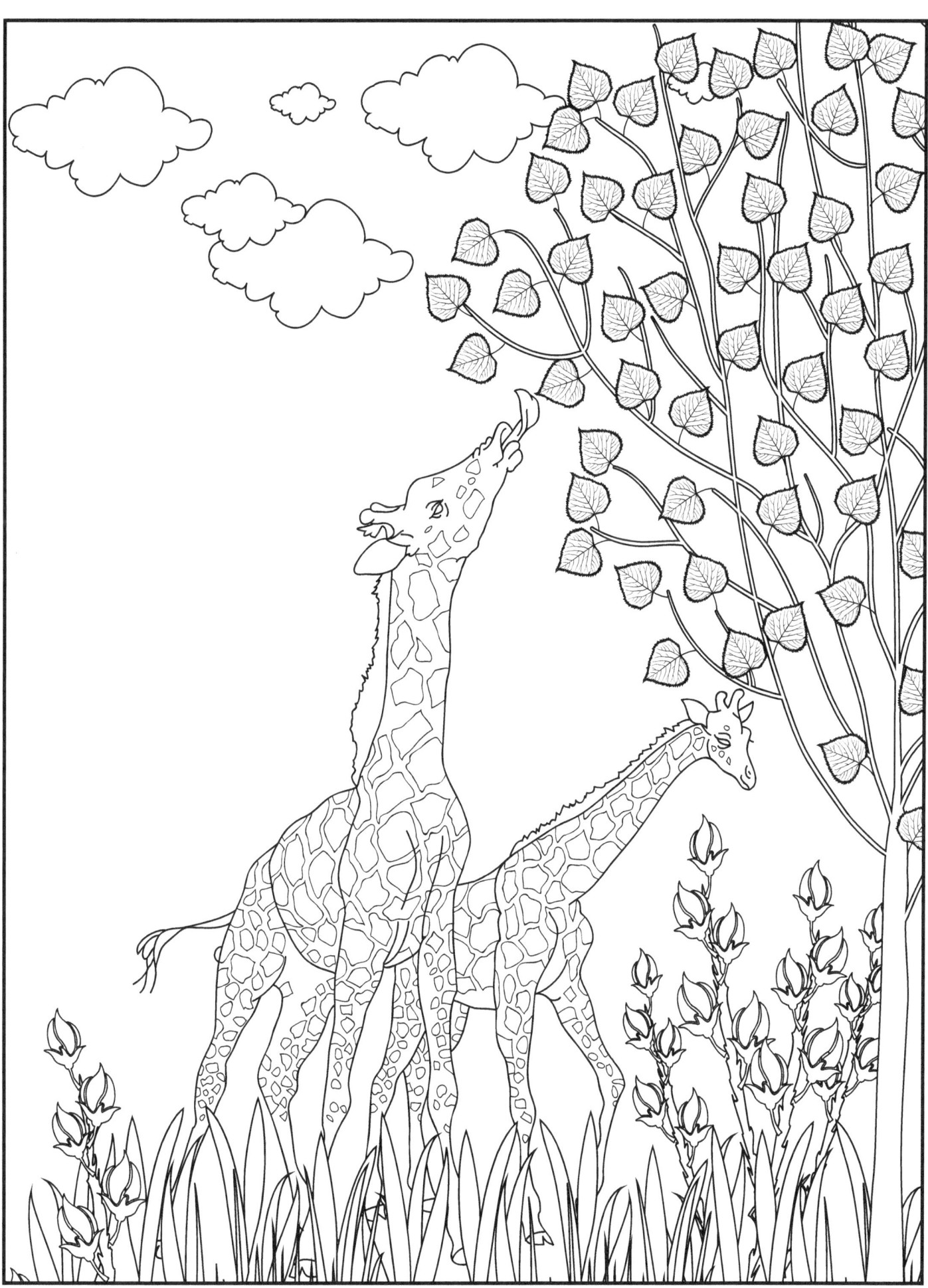

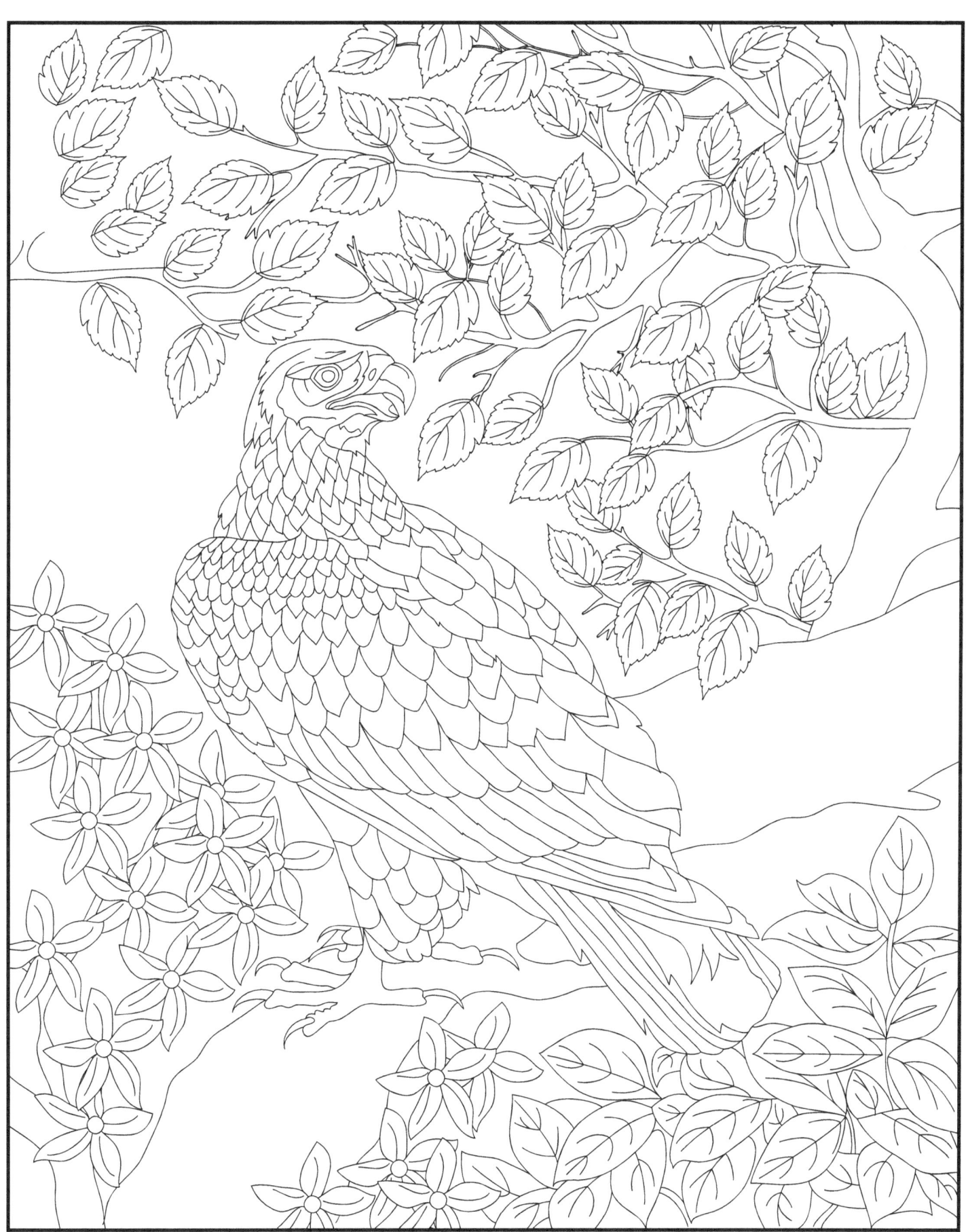

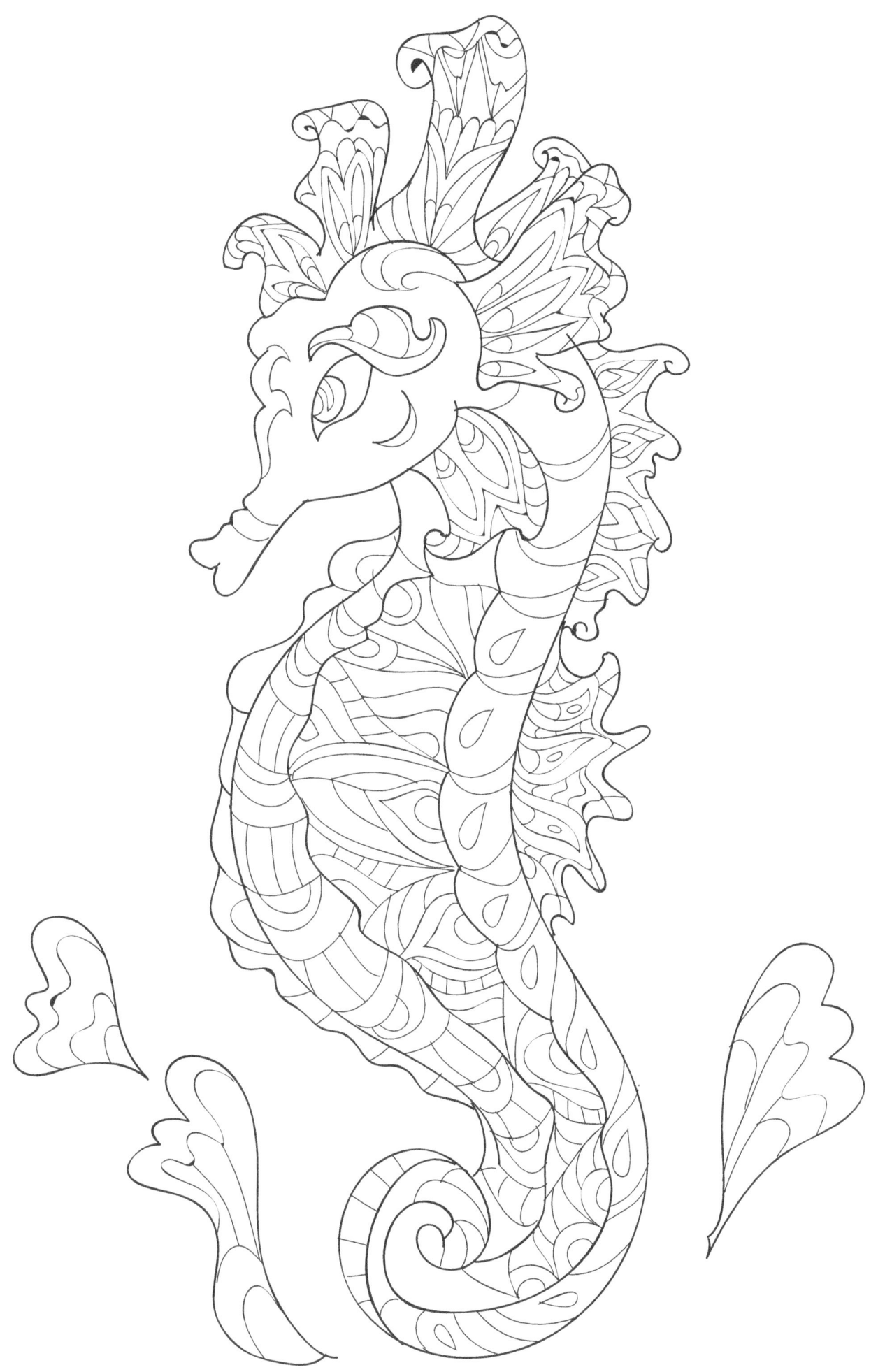

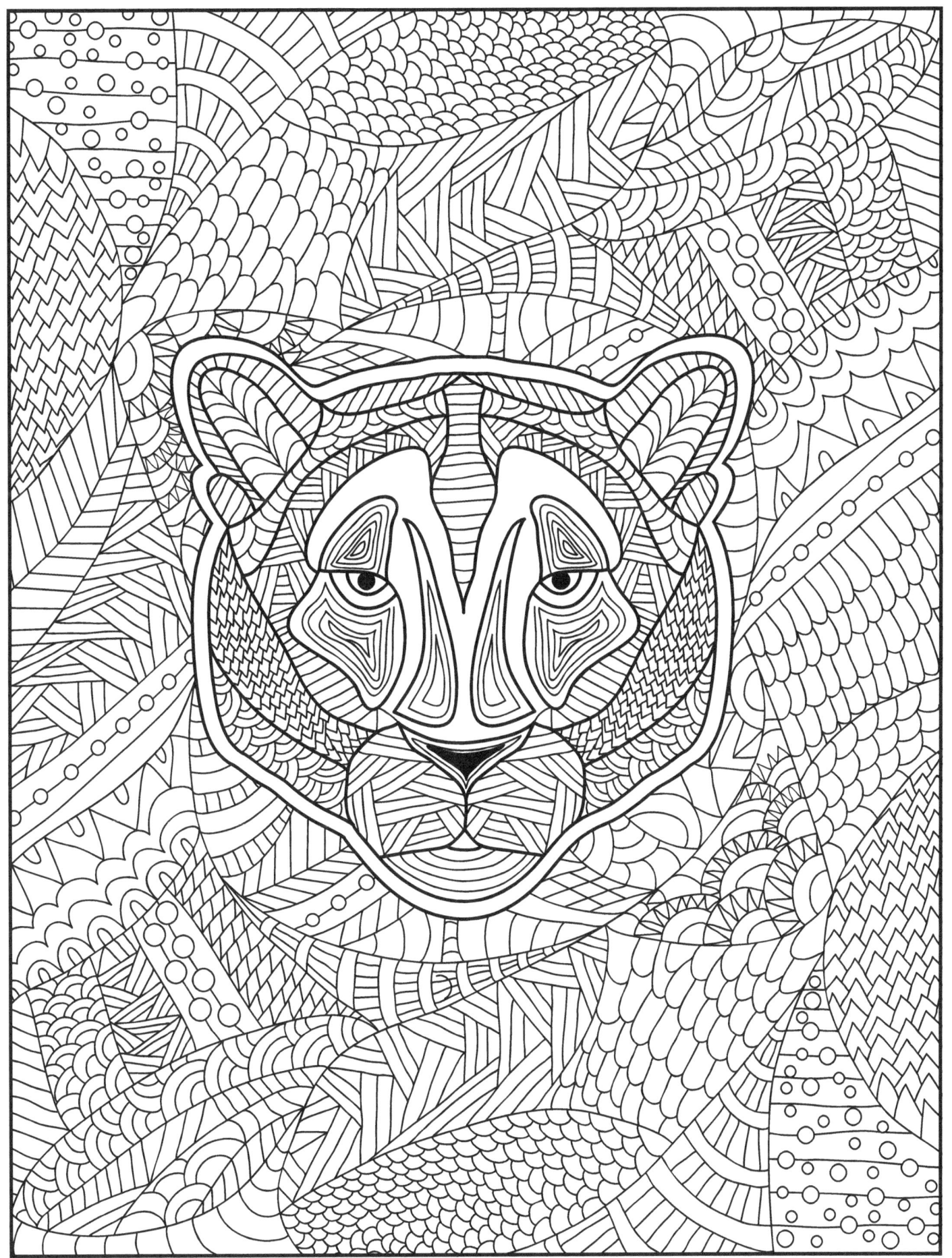

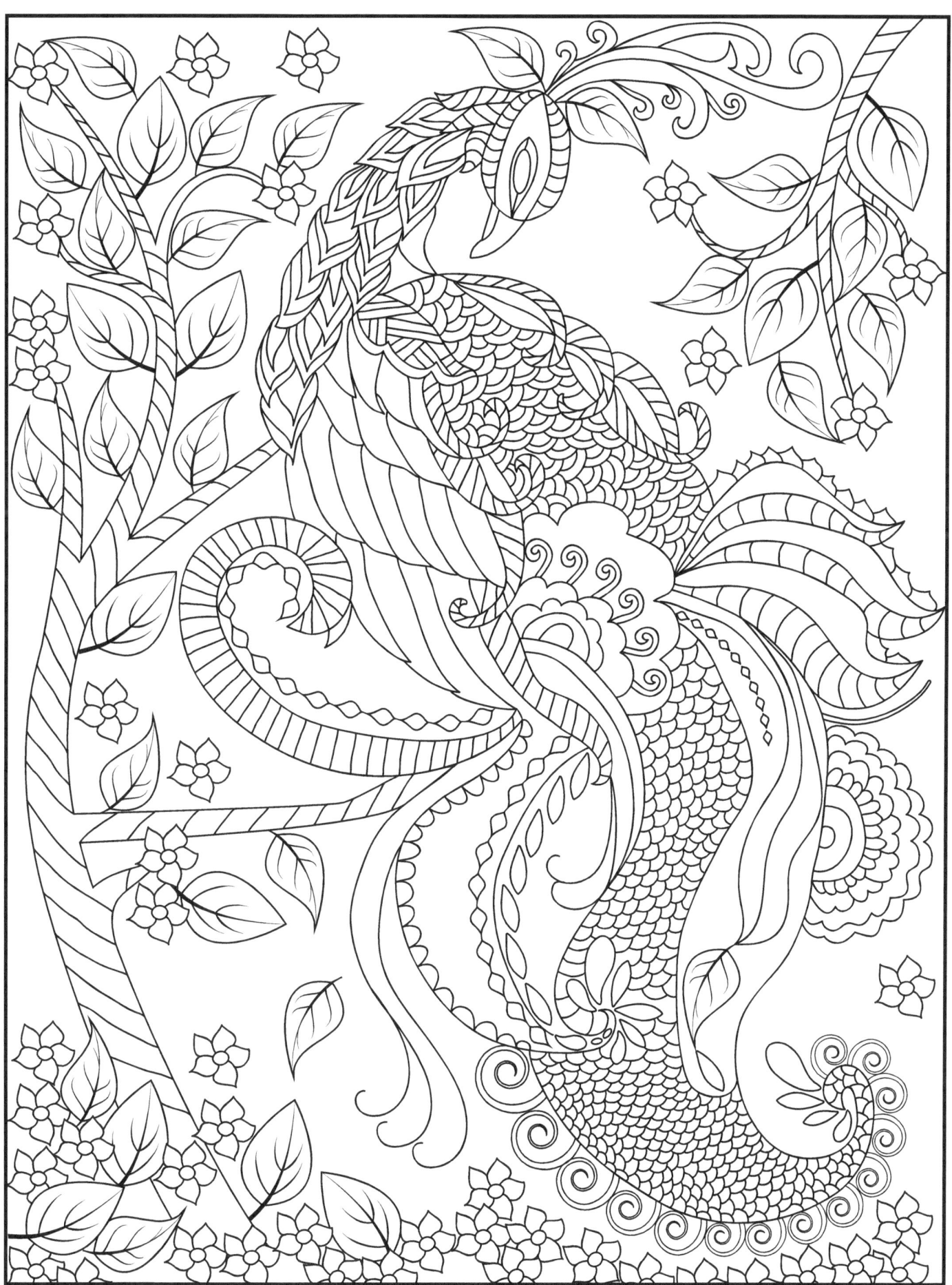

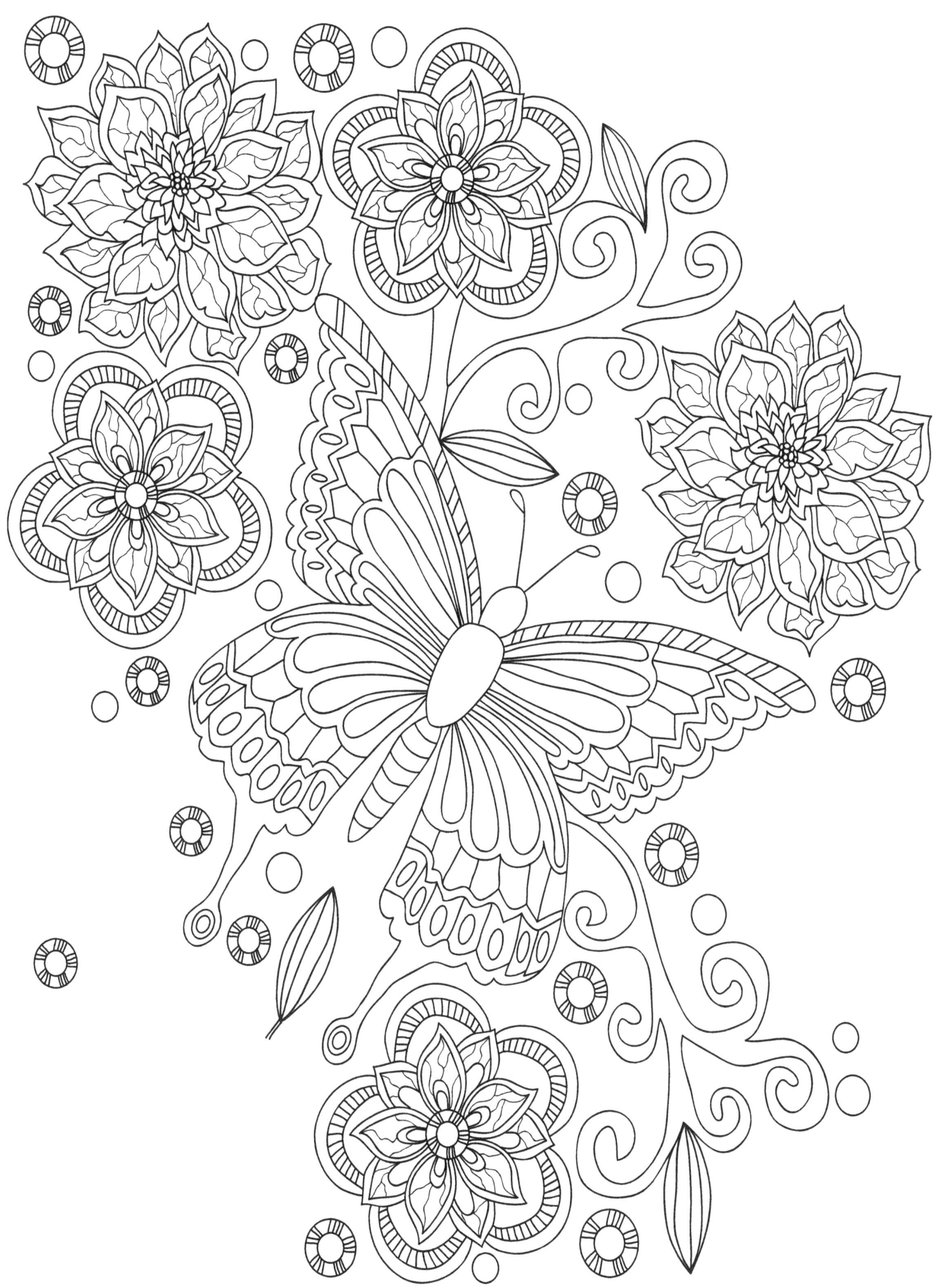

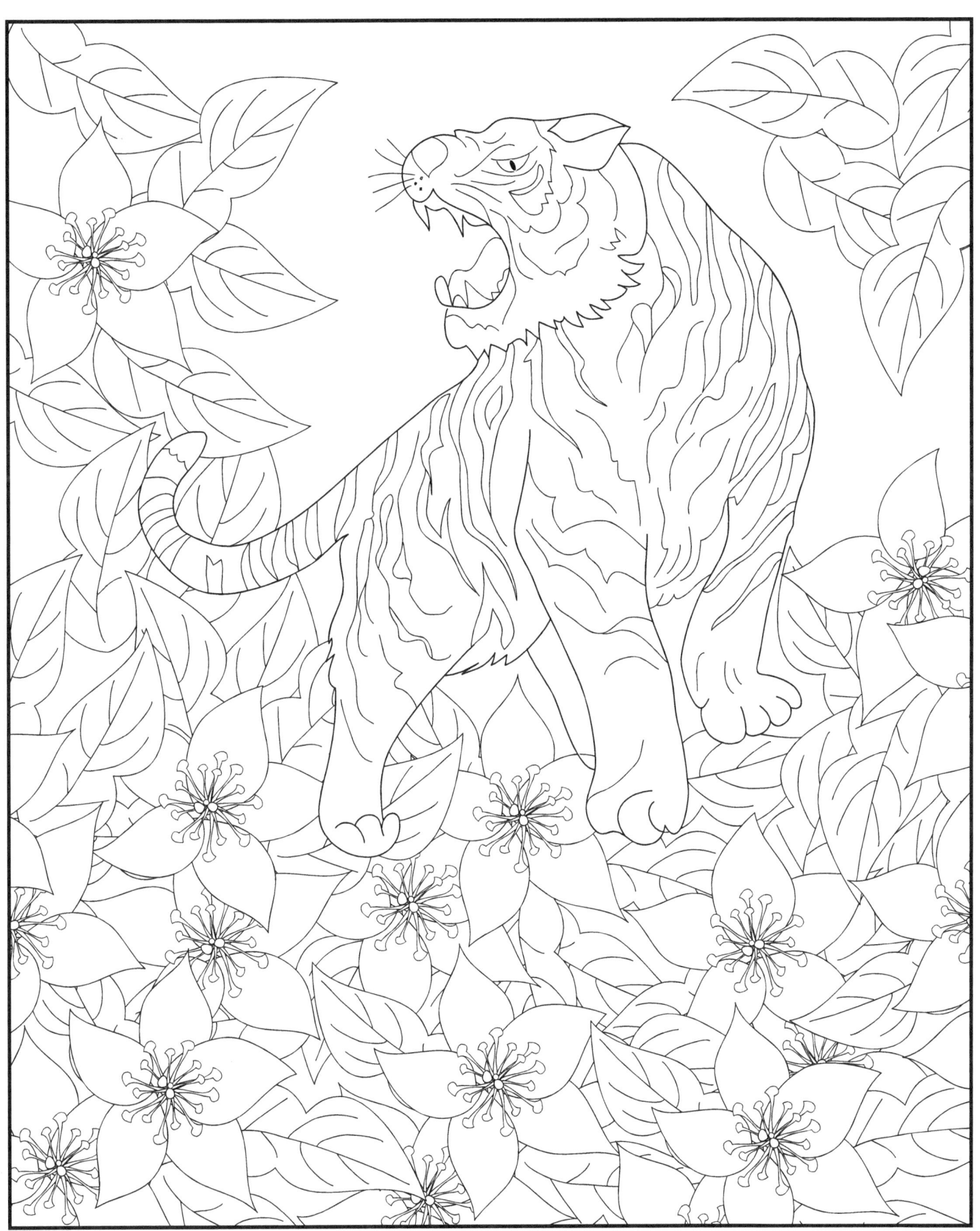

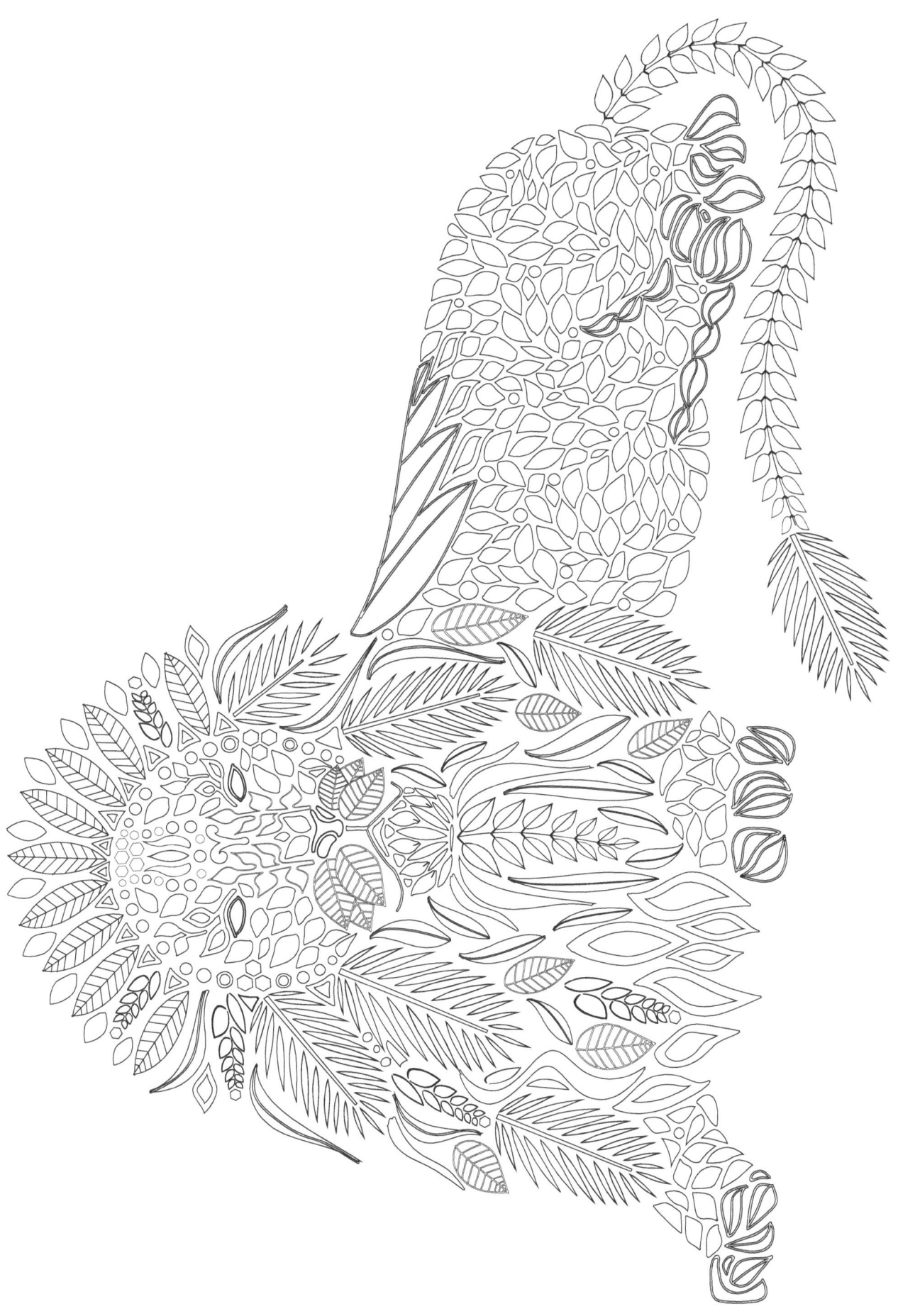

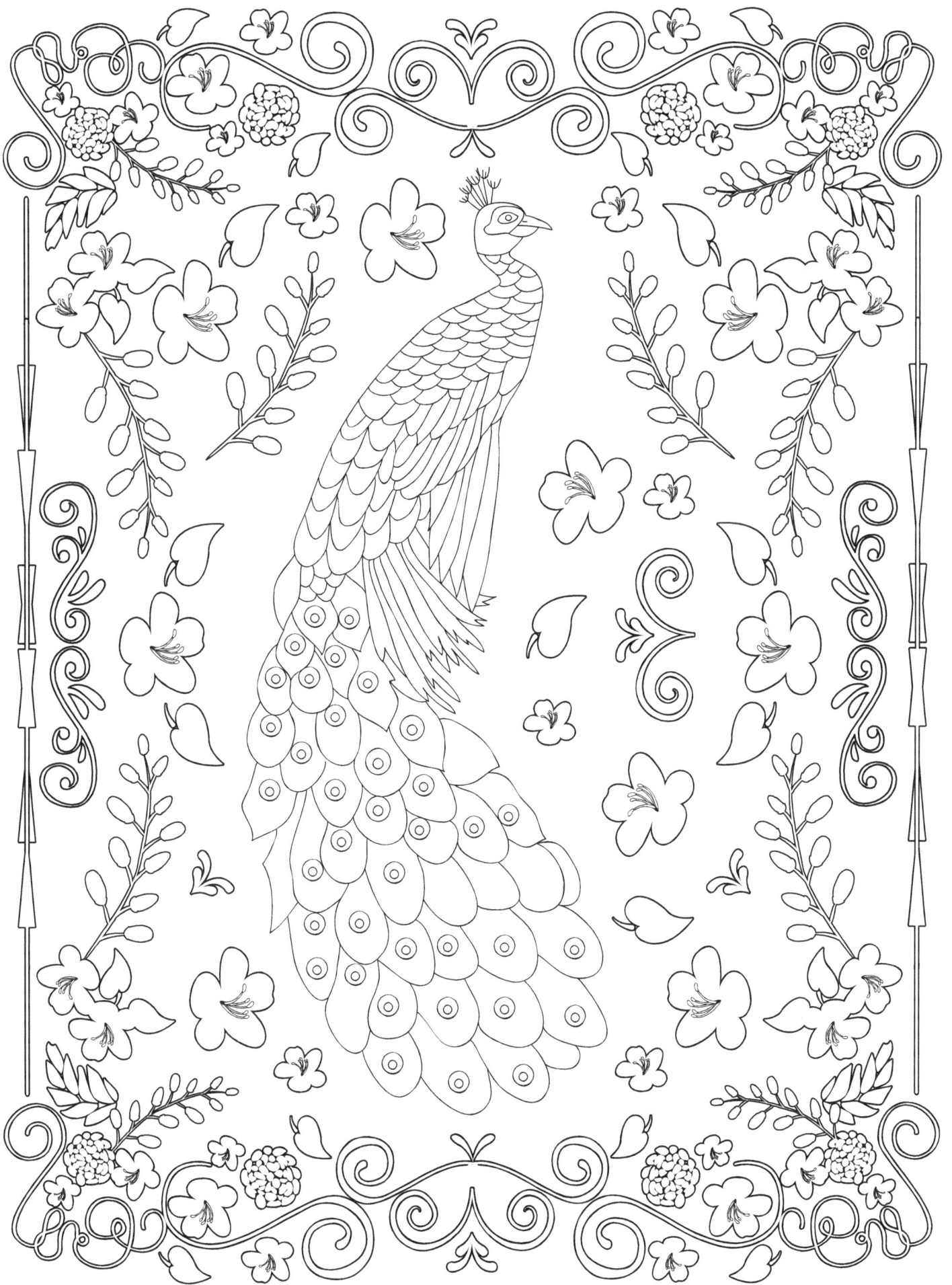

The end :)

We really hope you enjoyed this fun book!
Be sure to check out our other volumes coming soon
to Amazon and www.creativbooks.com.

www.ingramcontent.com/pod-product-compliance
Lightning Source LLC
Chambersburg PA
CBHW080943170526
45158CB00008B/2354